# Mathematics Around Us

John Blackwood

# Mathematics Around Us

Waldorf Education Resources

Floris Books

First published in 2006 by Floris Books
© 2006 John Blackwood

British Library CIP Data available

ISBN-10 0-86315-538-3
ISBN-13 978-086315-538-3

Produced by Polskabook, Poland

# Contents

# Introduction

In a recent article in the *Sydney Morning Herald* (20 Dec 2001) John Metcalfe of the Parent-controlled Christian Schools is quoted as saying 'Children are taught that maths is a language for describing the world — a language that God created ...'

This is something that I too have felt for many years now, and feel that it is an approach that can go far, very far, if taken with some seriousness. It assumes there is a secret to be revealed in the book of nature and that the world is far more than a long-term probabolistic accident, or calculable through embarrassingly huge extrapolations which no practical engineer would dream of making. One can, of course, permit oneself any number of views, after all there is no reason that *materialistic* science should have a monopoly on objectivity.

## Nominalism or the language of the gods?

One view is that the world of mathematics is a *nominalistic* and abstract collection of convenient ideas with little, if any, reality of their own and having mere convenience and pragmatic value in relation to understanding the world 'out there.' Although commented on by some thoughtful folk, the fact that mathematics is so *extraordinarily* good at this usually escapes our attention.

Another view is that mathematics is — in more senses than one — a language of the gods. It could be contended that what our minds apprehend in the concepts of mathematics and geometry is the last pale residue of the active forming forces that 'make the world happen.' The view held here does not assume that the thoughts we have are intellectual conveniences, mere shadows of the mind, but rather a veritable doorway towards a growing comprehension of the workshop of nature. One can take the view that, not only are there gods, but it is also possible to take an interest in *how* they work. This has been my attitude

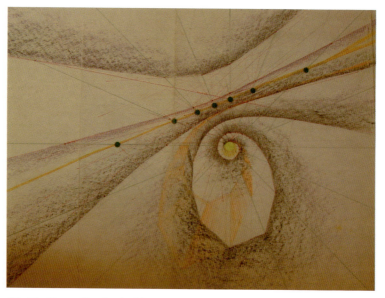

*Fig I.1  Generalized spiroid*

and I find myself affirmed in this through the sheer wonder of nature and the beauty of the subject we are dealing with. To me Shakespeare's 'pale cast of thought,' only applies to our current thin intellectuality, not to what the thought life might eventually achieve — as Rudolf Steiner has pointed out in his *Philosophy of Spiritual Activity*, 'with thinking we have grasped one small corner of the spiritual.'

No doubt there is a whole range of variations among these positions as well, and the whole thing could be debated endlessly. The amazement at the concordance of the mathematical concept with the carefully observed phenomenon can enable us to be very busy, intrigued and interested despite epistemological niceties — important though they no doubt are.

This book contains material from the main lessons I have given to Year 7. Each main lesson is done over approximately three weeks for one and a half hours each morning in our school, Glenaeon Rudolf Steiner School, in Australia.

Every teacher does these sessions differently and what is done ends up being unique to the group and to the teacher, to the place and to the time. However there seems to me to be a 'golden thread' to which we are all striving.

The Waldorf curriculum provides a constant challenge to every teacher. This challenge is to develop our work year by year for the sake of the students — and to develop ourselves through it too. I often wonder how we can expect our students to develop, work and grow if we ourselves are not striving to do the same. How can the kids grow if we are not? There has to be an equation here!

These notes are offered as a contribution to the mathematical themes.

I also thank the many students and friends whose work I have used in illustrations. Where they are known and accessible I have acknowledged this. My apologies if I cannot give personally all credit where credit is due.

It should hardly be necessary to suggest that these notes are only one individuals choice of material and that many would include quite other selections.

However, it is what I have worked with over some twenty-one years and it has been, over those years, of interest to some students and some colleagues — judging by the photocopies I have had to do!

John Blackwood
November 2005

# 1. Mathematics in Nature

At this beginning of puberty there is an increasing demand from the young folk to be able to connect the thoughts they can have *about* the world *with* the world they actually experience. Mathematics, and geometry in particular, can now be seen in much that surrounds us in the miracle that is nature. Something dawning inside us meets the phenomenon outside.

If there is a correspondence in the educative life of the children with the general growth and development of humanities consciousness then the historical period reflected is early and pre-Renaissance. This need to personally connect these two sides of life emerged for the individual at that time, and emerges strongly at puberty in the students' life too. The battle for autonomous thought was fraught with difficulty with the dominant faiths of the time deeming themselves under threat by individual efforts of the likes of Copernicus, Galileo and Kepler. The awakening mind of the young person also challenges *us* at this time!

We re-member at this time in the students' life the kind of work, approach and exploration just beginning to explode onto the world in Central Europe, and world-shaking and world-shaping it was — the Renaissance. But we need to do it out of where we are now.

What follows is a pictorial outline of some of the themes and topics that I did in a particular main lesson at Glenaeon Rudolf Steiner School many years ago in attempting to cover the kind of work I believed belonged to this age. Much else could be incorporated of course, and there is no pretence of completion, but this was some of the content offered at that time.

The pages which follow take typical exercises in the sequence that they were offered at the time. Sometimes there are suggestions as to accompanying activity and sometimes the initial sequence of steps of the work are indicated.

*Fig 1.1 The title page of the students' main lesson book should hint at the subsequent themes and contents for the three week main lesson*

## Review of some skills

We reviewed a couple of simple geometric constructions: bisecting an angle and drawing a line at right angles to another given line — just to get started.

This calls for compass and ruler. It always seems to me that careful use of the compass cannot be emphasized enough. A reasonable compass that does not wobble or skid, or widen spontaneously, as well as a sharp pencil, and a ruler with a clean edge (and not pockmarked by being banged against the edge of a desk) are essential. The ruler should be 30 cm long or more.

*Fig 1.2  Double rainbow over Sydney*

*Fig 1.3  Drawing a line perpendicular to another, bisecting an angle
— and a rainbow (compass work)*

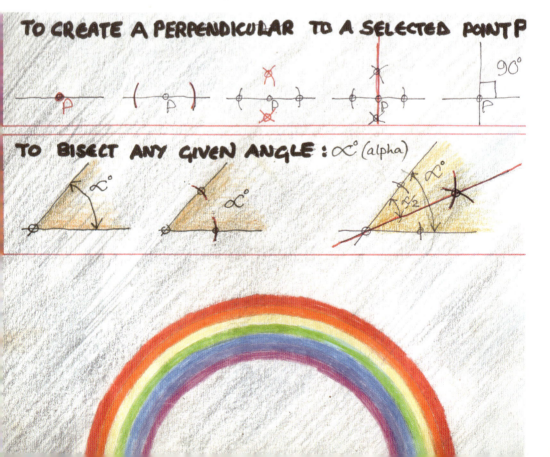

TO CREATE A PERPENDICULAR TO A SELECTED POINT P

90°

TO BISECT ANY GIVEN ANGLE: $\alpha°$ (alpha)

*Exercise 1   To draw a perpendicular to a given line*

1. Draw a line, *p,* and place on it a point, *P,* through which the perpendicular is to be struck.

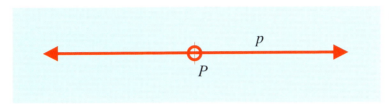

Fig 1.4

2. With a compass set at a radius of (say) 5 cm, and the pointy end set on *P,* mark the points, *A* and *B,* on either side of *P* as shown.

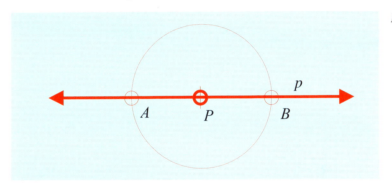

Fig 1.5

3. Now draw two arcs from *A* and *B* respectively, of a radius greater than 5 cm (say 7 cm) so that they intersect in *C* and *D.*

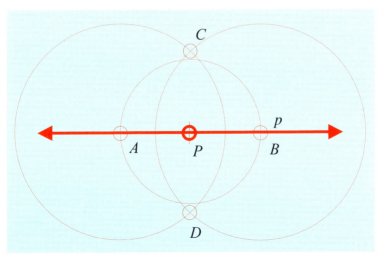

Fig 1.6

4. Join the points, *C* and *D*, and we have the line perpendicular to line *p* through the point *P* as required.

*Fig 1.7*

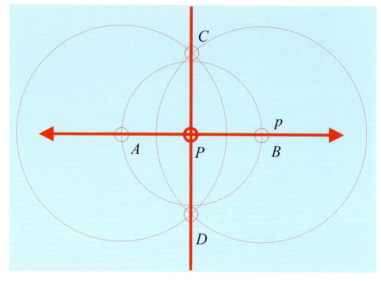

This is a further simple, but essential introductory exercise:

*Exercise 2    To bisect any given angle, α*

1. Draw two lines, *b* and *c*, intersecting in *A*, with α, the angle to be bisected (i.e. cut in half), between the two.

*Fig 1.8*

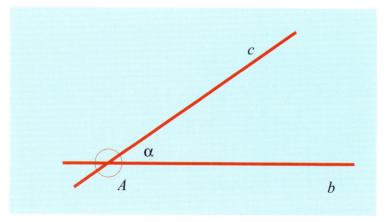

2. Select a radius, *AC,* of about 5 cm and set a compass to this radius. Put the compass point on point *A* and draw an arc creating points *B* and *C* on lines *c* and *b* respectively.

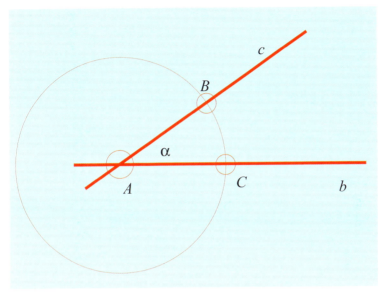

*Fig 1.9*

3. With compass at approximately the same radius draw arcs from *B* and *C* respectively to intersect at point *D*.

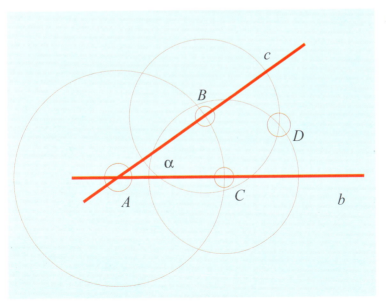

*Fig 1.10*

4. Finally, draw the line AD. This will be the required bisecting line, where $\angle BAD$ is equal to $\angle CAD$

i.e. $\angle BAD = \angle CAD = \beta$      hence $2\beta = \alpha$ as required.

*Fig 1.11*

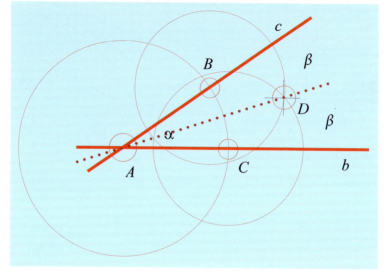

These above two constructions will be used in future diagrams and will only be referred to briefly if needed.

## Exercise 3   Rainbows

But what is out there in nature that has a patently geometric structure? Very many things if we look hard enough; and a delightful candidate often appears against dark shower clouds.

This third exercise approximates the rainbow. It is not easy to take photographs of these wonders as they span so much of the sky. But this is an excellent exercise in drawing concentric circles and then bringing the appropriate colours to them. Noted that red is on the *outside* of the inner bright (primary) rainbow and on the *inside* of the outer fainter (secondary) bow.

Conventionally there are the seven colours. Richard Of York Gained Battles In Vain is one mnemonic for the red, orange, yellow etc.

*Fig 1.12  A rainbow as semi-circle*

1. Set up a horizontal straight line.

2. Mark a point about its centre.

3. Set a compass at a radius about half the line length.

4. Scribe *eight* semi-circles (which means seven spaces) from the centre, where each radius is (say) 3 mm larger than the one before.

5. Colour between the circles!

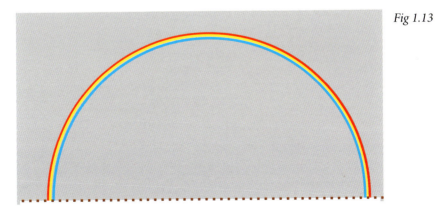

*Fig 1.13*

Do this on grey paper and finish with pastels — it can look startling. Above are only shown three such concentric circles attempting to partially emulate an actual rainbow as seen in Sydney early in the morning when the sun is low. To render this marvel to scale and with its magical luster is well nigh impossible.

## Circular forms

Where do we see circles? Drop a stone in a pond and circles of ripples emanate from the impact point as source.

### Exercise 4   Circles, from points and lines

We follow this rainbow drawing with an exercise that divides the circle into 16 divisions and which eventually appeared to give a series of concentric circles made from an array of near tangents.

1. First draw a line lightly across the paper through the middle *horizontally* and then, using the process described above for a right angle, construct a *vertical* line at 90° to it. Where they cross is point *O*.

*Fig 1.14*

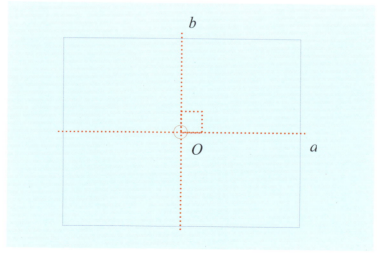

2. Bisect the right-angle on both sides. And bisect again all the eight new angles formed. This will create 16 divisions around the centre point, *O*. Now the angle between each line is

$$360 / 16 = 22.5°$$

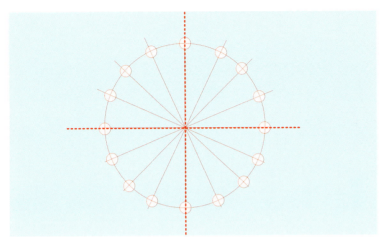

*Fig 1.15*

3. To obtain one of the concentric circles we now join (for example) every *fifth* point around the circle. It is easier to keep track if the points are numbered 1 through to 16.

4. Having done one such circle made from a family of (in this case) $2 \times 16 = 32$ lines, now try every sixth point and then every seventh and so on.

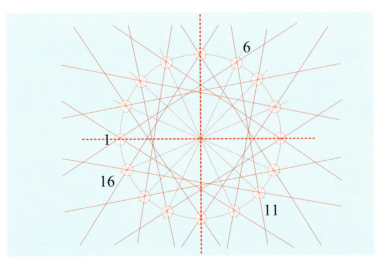

*Fig 1.16*

This will eventually lead to a family of approximate circles defined by series of tangents which are concentric to each other as is shown in Fig 1.17. It makes for an interesting picture if each resultant circle is formed of lines of a different colour. We thus obtain a *form* purely from a series of ordered lines. There will be more of this!

Note that the drawing indicates a suggestion of the lines not merely joining the points, but going *beyond* them. In essence a line is infinitely long, the two points merely defining its position:

Circles are everywhere, the whorl of the flower, the disc of the sun, the face of the moon, expanding ripples in the pond.

The next exercise explores this a little but it also enables us to see forms emerging that do not have the regularity of the circle but are still harmonious and symmetrical in themselves.

◄ *Fig 1.17 Concentric circles*

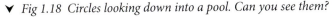

▼ *Fig 1.18 Circles looking down into a pool. Can you see them?*

*Exercise 5  Asymmetric forms*

The circle can be formed as in the exercise above (Exercise 4), but with a small modification of the construction, quite other forms can come about. Let us construct them first and then see if anything like them can to be seen around us.

1. Draw the perpendicular lines further *down* the page.

2. Now draw the equiangular radiants through point *O*. In this case 15° intervals have been chosen.

*Fig 1.19*

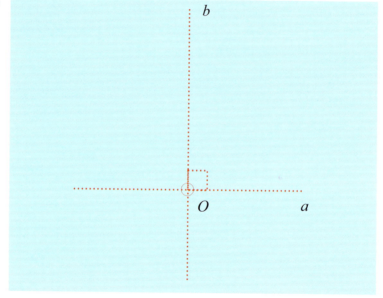

3. Then place a circle with its centre somewhat above the point *O*. Now mark and number (from 1 to 24) the points where the circle intersects the twelve radiants.

4. Join every fifth point with a line all the way across the drawing (see Fig 1.20). This will create the first curve.

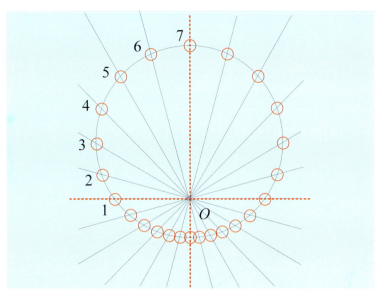

*Fig 1.20*

Then, as previously, join every second, third etc. point with a different colour: This gives a number of approximations to ovals formed from the tangent lines. A whole series of different *forms* appears.

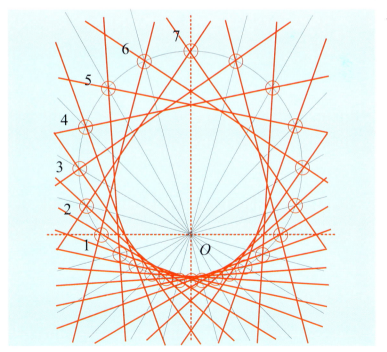

*Fig 1.21*

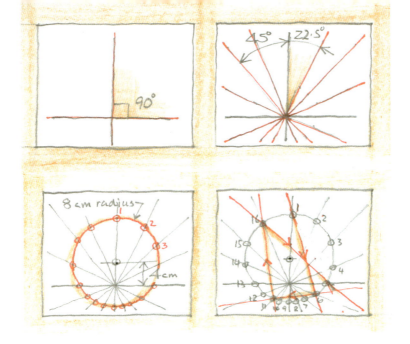

◀ Fig 1.22 Asymmetric oval form

▲ Fig 1.23 Constructing the ovals

5. The sketch in Fig 1.22 shows some of the whole family of these curves or ovals. Numerous constructions can follow as every 6, 7, 8, 9 etc. points can be joined. Within the centred circle these lines formed concentric circles (as we saw in Fig 1.17). But, when the circle is offset as in this case, a field of nested ovals emerges and it is interesting to challenge the students to see if they can discover any kind of order *outside* the circle. Teachers should try it first.

Note that with *even* numbered points you will have to have more than one starting point to get the full form. Odd numbers will eventually come back to the same starting point.

Do we see such ovals about us anywhere? The shapes look a bit like ellipses. Leaving aside whether they actually *are* ellipses for the moment we note that some egg forms look to all external appearances, very close to these.

The emu egg profile is a case in point. Accurate analysis shows it is close but not quite. Other eggs can be close too, and not just bird eggs. Local fauna in Australia, both platypus and echidna have nearly elliptical egg forms. This is a study in itself. Suffice to say that here is an obvious kinship between the phenomenon of an egg and conceptually devised oval (see Fig 1.24).

*Fig 1.24 Emu egg and an ellipse*

Still staying with the circle as a beginning it may be of value to see what happens when the circle is divided into six. Are there representatives of a sixfold character in nature? Little doubt about this one!

## Hexagonal forms

We drew a number of examples of sixfold symmetry. The students should be encouraged to find their own examples as much as possible. It can be amazing what a resource the class can be when many eyes (including parents and friends) are out there looking!

The basic hexagon is simple to construct. Bees are doing it all the time, so much so that artificial foundation for the cells in the

*Fig 1.25  Hexagons galore!*

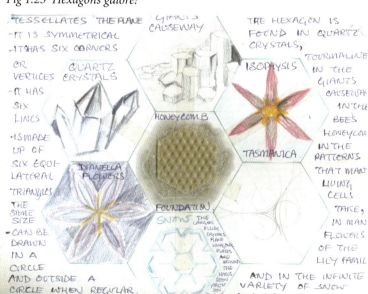

hive can be made from stampings in beeswax and the bees will use it. Having had bees myself, it is fascinating to watch how the bees will build their cells both with and without the artificial foundation. Quartz crystals often show a good six-fold symmetry. Many flowers, especially the lily family, exhibit this closely as does the sun orchid flower of New South Wales.

*Fig 1.26 –28 Hexagons in crystal, flower petal and beeswax layout*

What do we do with compass, pencil and ruler to construct a regular hexagon? Easy.

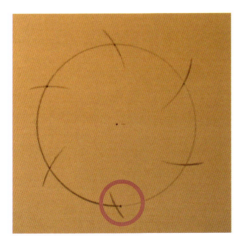

*Fig 1.29 Checking our accuracy!*

A good check on one's own accuracy is to start at any point on a circle, with the compass point. It is an accurate drawer that makes it so that the last arc does not overshoot or undershoot the original point! Try it.

*Exercise 6   Constructing a regular hexagon*

1. Draw a circle, centre *O*, with a radius of about 5 cm. Draw a horizontal line through *O*, and mark the intersections of line and circle *AB*.

2. With compass set on point *A*, and retaining the circle radius, mark two arcs on the circle. Do the same from the point *B* as well.

3. Join *A* to *C* to *D* to *B* to *E F* to *A* and we have the hexagon.

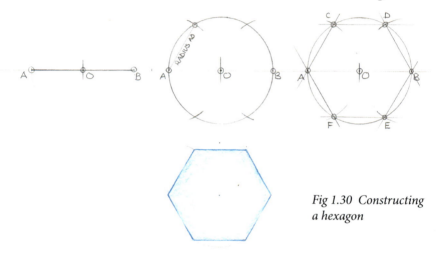

Fig 1.30  Constructing
a hexagon

*Exercise 7   Making a snowflake*

Another hexagonal form, which emphasizes the sixfold symmetry in nature is a snowflake.

1. To make a paper 'snowflake' take a thin A4 (letter) sheet of plain white paper and with compass draw a circle about 8 cm radius.

2. Construct a regular hexagon as in Exercise 6.

Fig 1.31

3. Cut out the hexagon neatly.

4. Now fold along a *diameter.*

5. Then fold to other corners until an equilateral triangle is formed.

6. From the point, or corner, which is at the centre of the original hexagon, imagine a line to the lower outer edge bisecting the 60° angle at the centre and fold again. This should leave a right-angled triangle.

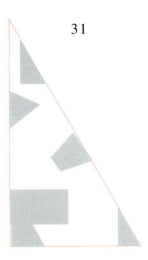

*Fig 1.32  Typical cut-out*

7. On the sides cut away the paper in any way you choose to mimic a snowflake (see Bentley and Humphreys amazing book *Snow Crystals,* for a large variety of snowflake photographs).

8. Unfold all the triangles, taking care not to tear the paper, and we have a great big 'snowflake'! The students usually love this one.

*Fig 1.33  Snowflake through cutaway paper*

## Spiral forms

Such exercises as the above let us see that in natural shapes there are mirrored what we can imagine in our minds geometrically, or mathematically. Does this mean the 'mathematics' is inherent in the expressions and widths of nature? Can it be otherwise? Are ideas mere nominal abstractions? Perhaps questions for later! It is certainly a question asked by many a scientist.

In the first instance the forms are simple and easily constructed. Now we come to forms which are *curved* in particular ways. Are such forms out there in nature all around us as well? Consider first a simple spiral.

## Archimedes spiral

The spiral of Archimedes could also be called the rope spiral (or the geometry of the raffia place mat). This is a spiral which is easily made with a piece of string. Start by holding one end of the string or rope, and wind a tight circle around until the string overlays the held end, and keep on and on winding.

This spiral has the characteristic that for each full turn the spiral gets larger by the *same* amount each time. It has a linear character. It increases stepwise forever — if the rope (or raffia) is long enough!

*Figs 1.34, 35  Rope stay for cannon — an Archimedean spiral*

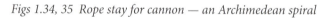

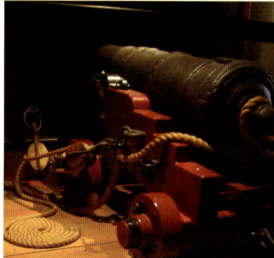

*Exercise 8   Spiral of Archimedes*

This spiral can be drawn by the students as shown.

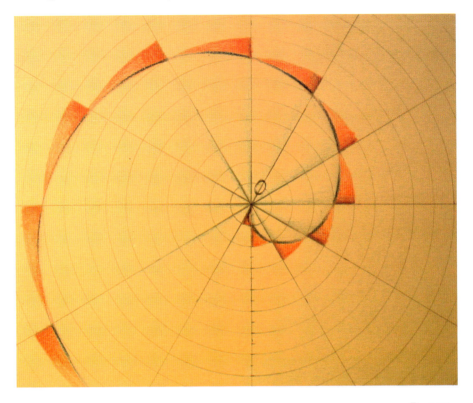

*Fig 1.36*

1. Draw vertical and horizontal axes.

2. With centre *O* draw concentric circles increasing in (say) 5 mm steps.

3. Draw radial lines every 30° (say) around *O*.

4. Now, starting at the centre, draw alternately steps out *radially,* and then around each arc for 30° step, then radially again and around and so on, alternately.

This was one particular and well-defined spiral. But it is not actually common in nature, as far as I can tell. If you find such a spiral, please share it with me.

*Exercise 9   Spirals galore*

At this point it might be good to look around and see if the students can find the *general* spiral form in as many artifacts as possible. A very few samples are shown here. Make sketches.

The students should look to see how many examples they can find round about them, and then sketch them, from seashells to galaxies, water vortices to a head of hair (do men and women, boys and girls, differ in this one?).

*Fig 1.40  Vortex*

*Fig 1.37  Tunisian snail
shell (Terry Funk)*

*Fig 1.38  Epitonum
species sea shell*

*Fig 1.39  Ammonite
from Frieberg*

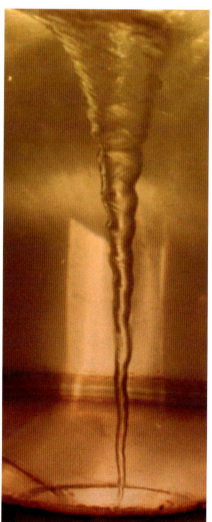

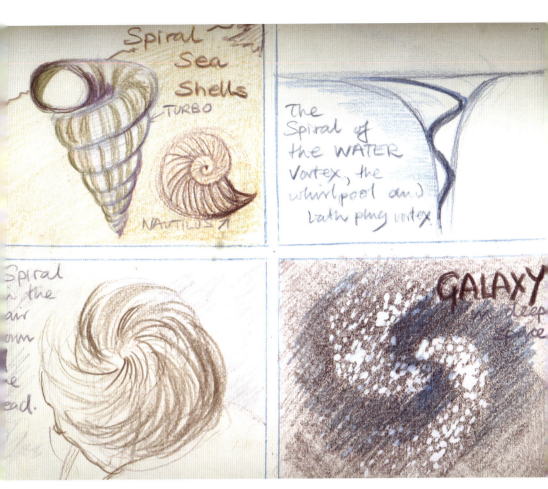

Spiral
Sea
Shells
TURBO
NAUTILUS

The
Spiral of
the WATER
Vortex, the
whirlpool and
bath plug vortex.

Spiral
in the
air
own
e
ead.

GALAXY
in deep
space

*Fig 1.41*

## The equiangular spiral

There are a number of other kinds of spiral. One is the *equi-angular* or *logarithmic* spiral. Interestingly a simple example of the equiangular spiral can be drawn by working with hexagons again as we see a little later. So we build with circles and hexagons. But we need a couple of preliminary construction methods.

*Exercise 10   Bisecting a line segment*

We will need a method to bisect a given line segment. This can, of course, be done with a ruler by measurement but it is geometrically more elegant to use the construction shown here using compass and straight edge, and it is a useful skill to have.

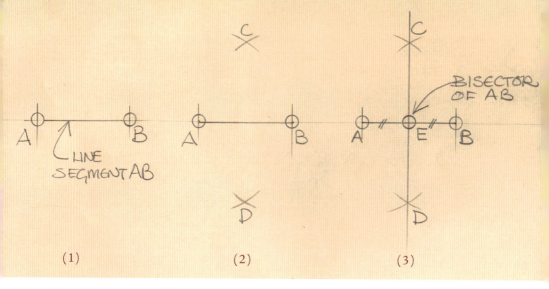

Fig 1.42 Bisection of a line segment

1. Draw the line segment, *AB*, which it is desired to bisect.

2. Set a compass at a radius approximately equal to the distance *AB*. Describe arcs at *A* and *B* so that they intersect at points *C* and *D*.

3. Now join points *C* and *D* and note where this line crosses *AB*. This is the point *E* which is placed so that *AE* is equal to *EB*, hence bisecting *AB* as required.

*Exercise 11   An equiangular spiral through a series of hexagons*

We now construct a series of hexagons, one within the other, getting smaller and smaller but in an ordered fashion. One could of course go the other way and draw larger and larger hexagons too, for the series goes on indefinitely, getting larger outwardly and getting smaller inwardly — never in fact actually reaching the centre.

1. Draw a circle of (say) 10 cm radius. On this circle construct a hexagon as shown in an earlier exercise (Exercise 6).

2. Bisect each of the six sides (Exercise 10).

3. Join these six bisecting points with six lines. This forms another, smaller hexagon. Bisect the sides of this new smaller hexagon.

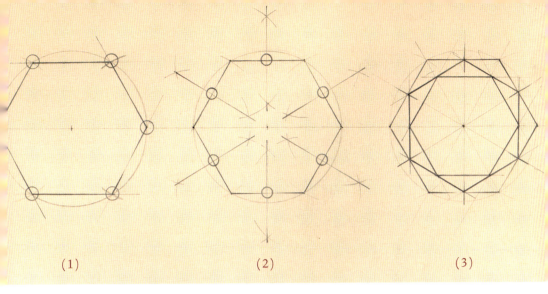

(1)              (2)              (3)

*Fig 1.43  Constructing a hexagon, bisecting the sides, constructing a further hexagon, and so on alternately. The hexagons get smaller and smaller.*

4. Join these midpoints and we have a third, yet smaller, hexagon.

5. Now pick out the *isosceles* triangles as they decrease in size going in an anticlockwise direction as shown in Fig 1.44.

6. Continue this process a number of times as the triangles approach the centre of the original circle. The sequence of triangles forms an easily constructed equiangular spiral, and many can be seen in the same diagram.

Various ways of further elaboration can give interesting effects. The students usually amaze us with their imagination.

*Fig 1.44  A family of equiangular spirals*

The more general (algebraic) expression for such a spiral is a little more complicated. Developing these expressions belongs to analytic geometry that we do in Year 11. It is interesting that the first set of coordinates we come to in *this* Year 7 main lesson are *polar coordinates* — although this is left unsaid as far as the students are concerned.

We notice that our spirals, the one derived from decreasing hexagons, and the more general expression, both attempt to converge upon the centre of the diagram.

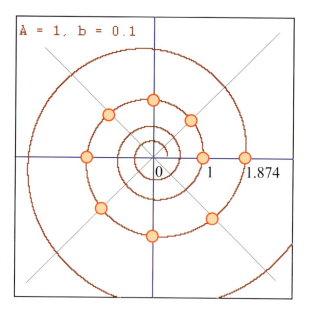

*Fig 1.45 An equiangular or logarithmic spiral using a True Basic program*

As the hexagons decrease it becomes harder and harder to draw them. The point to notice is that, mentally, we can *imagine* them (sort of) continuing forever, towards *a point at infinity,* on the page, but never seeming to be able to reach it. So we have what could be called a *local* infinitude.

For the general expression $r = Ae^{b\theta}$ it would be the same. If we programme a computer to plot this curve and simply let it run with continually *decreasing* values (i.e. negative) for $\theta$ it should never stop! (My program eventually comes up with 'overflow' if I don't limit it).

Likewise for *increasing* hexagons and angle $\theta$, the spirals would expand outwards indefinitely. This says something quite important, and to hint at it to the younger students, namely that the geometric drawings we do are no more than fragments and actually imply that such drawings (in our minds at least) span the entire infinite. This actually applies to *all* geometric drawings, and in a certain way it means we can never draw a complete geometric drawing! Older students learn to *use* this idea. We can, after all, only try to *imagine* a line, for instance, at infinity. Now *that* is being holistic!

Do we see such spirals around us? Yes! Students need to look, find and share their discoveries in this area. A few examples are shown here including the famous nautilus, a shell used almost as an icon in this and other design work!

*Fig 1.46 Nautilus section*

Look along the axis of any cone shell and we see the spiral form. It is interesting to note that most cone sea-shells have a particular handedness or chirality.

*Exercise 12  Chirality or handed-ness check for sea shells*

1. Find examples of 'right-hand' spirals (that is, starting from the centre these turn clockwise). Are many sea shells dextrose, or right-handed? Check all the sea shells you can find. The answer may surprise you.

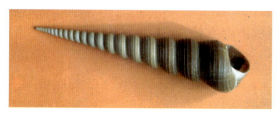

*Fig 1.47  Right-hand spiral shell. Start from the pointy end and ask: which way do I have to turn to go along the spiral of the shell away from me?*

2. Find examples of 'left-hand' spirals (that is, starting from the centre these turn anticlockwise).

Can you find any? Get the students to look — hard! For there are *very* few out there. The lightning whelk (*Busycon perversum*), a sea shell from the Gulf of Mexico, Yucatan, is one of the very few left-handers.

*Fig 1.48*  Busycon perversum — *left-hand spiral  (JB)*

There are few exceptions. Ask the students to look through any book on sea shells and see if they find *any* anticlockwise (or left-hand) spirals. They will find very few. Why this is the case is still a mystery.

Further examples are a beautiful pyrites fossil from Russia, an opalised spiral shell and an operculum shell, often seen on beaches around Sydney, Australia.

*Fig 1.49  Opalised shell (from Ann Jacobsen)*

*Fig 1.50  Operculum or trapdoor of a Turbo shell (from a local beach in Sydney)*

*Fig 1.51  Pyrites fossil (from David Bowden)*

In what follows we find that often we can see *interacting* spirals, both clockwise and anticlockwise for spirals appear in much more than only sea-shells.

First we look, though, at specific number sequences and slowly build a picture of spirals in the plant world.

As the hexagons get smaller, they decrease in the *same proportion*. That is, we multiply each successive diameter by the *same* number (less than 1). This is called the *common ratio* and defines a particular kind of sequence. However, there are other kinds of series which have particular importance in nature.

## Fibonacci numbers and sequences

One is the famous Fibonacci sequence. This was given by Fibonacci in about 1202 in his treatise *Liber abaci* concerning rabbits. And goes like this:

1,   1,   2,   3,   5,   8,   13,   21,   34,   55,   89 .......

*What is the next term after 89? Find the next five terms and state an expression for any term $F_n$ where n is the next term after the two terms* n – 1 *and* n – 2.

*Exercise 13   Fibonacci numbers — the celery stick and others*

Where do we observe these Fibonacci numbers occurring in our world? In very many places actually. The humble celery stick, if a section is cut near the ground, hints at two different spirals, *one* in one direction and *two* in the other, *between* the flesh of the stems and thus demonstrating an instance of two consecutive Fibonacci numbers 1 and 2.

The spirals, interestingly, are what are *not* there materially, but *between* the flesh of the stalks. There is a big story here somewhere ....

Many plants have two sets of spirals — one clockwise the other anticlockwise, sometimes hard to see. The numbers of these spirals are often consecutive Fibonacci numbers.

One can make a 'print' of the celery section quite easily. Try it.

1. Obtain fresh celery plant.

2. Section horizontally the stick of celery with a sharp knife near the base.

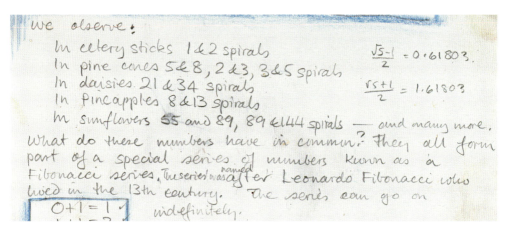

We observe:

In celery sticks 1 & 2 spirals
In pine cones 5 & 8, 2 & 3, 3 & 5 spirals
In daisies 21 & 34 spirals
In pineapples 8 & 13 spirals
In sunflowers 55 and 89, 89 & 144 spirals — and many more.
What do these numbers have in common? They all form part of a special series of numbers known as a Fibonacci series. The series was named after Leonardo Fibonacci who lived in the 13th century. The series can go on indefinitely.

$\frac{\sqrt{5}-1}{2} = 0.61803$

$\frac{\sqrt{5}+1}{2} = 1.61803$

$0 + 1 = 1$

*Fig 1.52  Finding the Fibonacci series*

3. Hold the stems reasonably firmly and 'ink' or paint the cross section with solid colour. Carefully wipe off excess colour.

4. Now, on clean paper, make a 'print' of the section. It should look something like Fig 1.53.

*Fig 1.53  Celery cross section print*

Note that the colour shows up where the plant flesh is *not* but indicates its structure (or form). You may have to try this a few times! And then seek the double spiral. It is not easy to see ....

*Fig 1.54  Grass trees — Xanthorea australis*


Also the cross section of the *grass tree*, made just after fire, shows a strong suggestion of interacting spirals.

See if the students (and teacher!) can figure out how many there are and which way they are going. Again it is not easy.

*Fig 1.55  Grass tree section after a fire*

## Fibonacci spirals

The above are only two examples hinting at a hidden order. To mirror what nature appears to be doing we can find a way to construct such spirals geometrically. A very neat way is described quite fully by Peter Stevens in his book *Patterns in Nature*. The method we have used here for Fig 1.56 follows in the next major exercise.

### Exercise 14   Constructing a pair of Fibonacci spirals

Suppose we want to construct *five* equispaced spirals in a clockwise direction (yellow) and *three* in an anticlockwise direction (red) as in Fig 1.56.

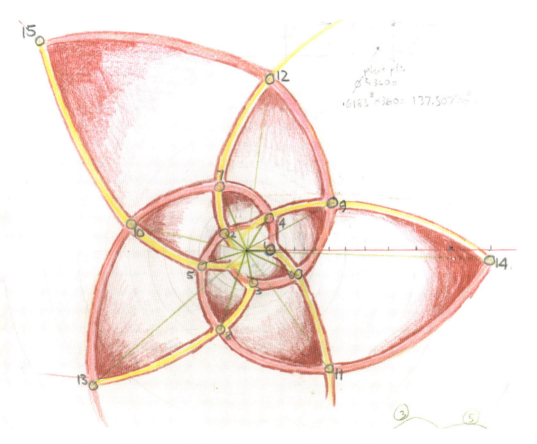

*Fig 1.56  Five spirals clockwise from centre and three anticlockwise*

1. Draw a horizontal line across the middle of the paper. On the centre of this line lightly mark a point *O*. Draw a circle 10 mm radius with *O* as centre.

2. We now draw a series of concentric circles about *O*. The radii about *O* are determined by what we call a 'multiplier' or common ratio, common because it is used again and again. In this case we could use 1.2 as our multiplier. Starting with a radius of 10 mm, to calculate the next term, we simply multiply by 1.2, (i.e. $10.00 \times 1.2 = 12$) and then 1.2 again and again. Hence the first few radii are:

   10
   12
   14.4
   17.28
   20.736
   24.8832
   29.85984
   35.831808
   42.99816960
   51.59780352
   61.91736422
   74.30083706
   89.16100448
   106.99322053
   128.3918464

3. Since we can hardly draw with pencil and ruler to much better than half a millimetre we could have rounded off as we went for our calculator usually retains the accuracy whether set to round off or not. We need to go to a radius of about 100 mm and round off to *one* decimal place as below.

   10.0
   12.0
   14.4
   17.3
   20.7

24.9
29.9
35.8
43.0
51.6
61.9
74.3
89.2
107.0
128.4

4. Draw concentric circles with all these radii, centre *O*, to cover the page. This is a good compass accuracy practice for this age group.

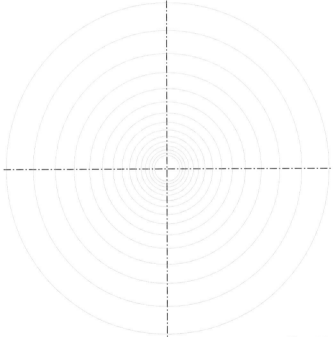

*Fig 1.57*

5. The next step will have to await proper justification until later. Suffice for the moment to say that, just as we can have a Golden section or ratio, so is it possible to have a Golden angle. The Golden section is explored a little later. Now we use the Golden angle itself. This angle is very close to 137.5° (the exact value can be calculated as shown in the panel — for those interested).

*Golden angle*

Assume the Golden section is

$$(\sqrt{5} + 1)/2 = 1.618033989...$$

as far as most school calculators will go. Now divide the full circle of 360° by this number i.e.,

$$360°/1.618033989 = 222.4922359°$$

and subtract this from 360°. This gives 137.577640° and this, to half a degree, is 137.5°. This is the angle we require, as the ratios of the angles about a point centre are:

$$360° \; : \; 222.4922359° \; : \; 137.577640°$$
$$1.618033989 \; : \; 1 \; : \; 0.618033989$$
$$(\sqrt{5} + 1)/2 \; : \; 1 \; : \; (\sqrt{5} - 1)/2$$

or, in words, the ratio of the whole to the larger part is the same as the ratio of the larger to the smaller part.

We could use a normal protractor now, starting from the horizontal line and marking sequentially anticlockwise lines from the centre. But it is far easier to make a single paper angle 'protractor' of 137.5° and step around the centre with this angle, drawing rays to the periphery of the drawing with each anticlockwise turn of this Golden angle.

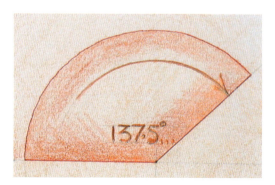

*Fig 1.58 Golden angle 'protractor'*

6. Starting from the smallest 10 mm radius circle, mark a point, on the horizontal line right of centre, where the radius cuts the circle. Mark this as point 1. Then point 2 will be the intersection of the circle with radius 12 mm and the line at $1 \times 137.5°$ anticlockwise from the centre. Point 3 will be the intersection of the circle with radius 14.4 mm and the line at $2 \times 137.5°$ anticlockwise from the centre. And so on, round and round in an anticlockwise direction ... continue until you have run out of points (there were 15 calculated) or have covered the page!

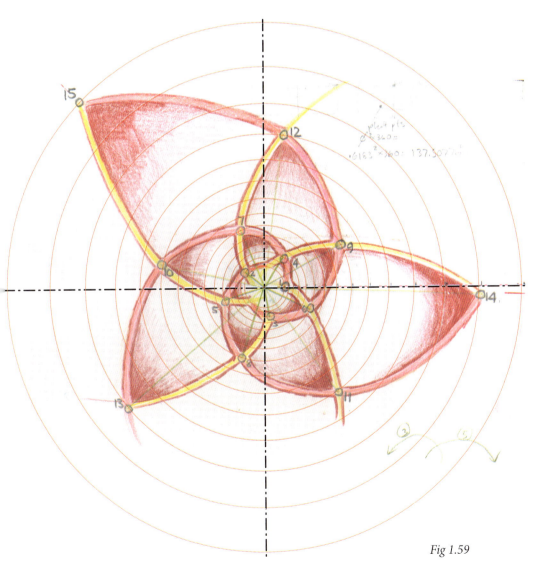

*Fig 1.59*

7. To obtain the spirals themselves we join a series of the numbered points. One series is used for the three anticlockwise spirals and a different series for the five clockwise spirals. For the five clockwise spirals join points (5, 10 and 15) and (2, 7 and 12), (4, 9 and 14) and (1, 6 and 11) and finally (3, 8 and 13). Note these are sequences of every *five* points.

For the three anticlockwise spirals we join three sequences of every *three* points. Mark both series of spirals in lightly.

8. Finally firm in, in free hand, the curves themselves as below. Do it for yourself first before leading Class 7 through this exercise.

*Fig 1.60*

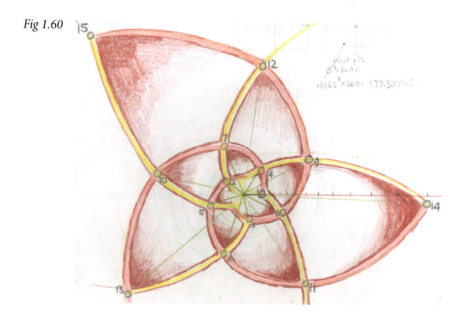

Note, that as for the celery section, we can fill in the areas *between* the spirals. In some plant forms it is suggested that it is what is *filled in* that we see physically. It is the mind's eye that discerns the *spiral* architecture as such, for we are actually describing something that is not materially manifest. For me it is enough however, in this case, that the students see and draw the beauty of the forms.

We have seen how this Fibonacci series of numbers is glimpsed in the way related to spirals in plant form. We can even draw such spirals. Another appearance is in the human body

*Fig 1.61  Golden ratio dividers (model by Roger McHugh)*

where certain proportions approximate to a particular number that is intimately related to this peculiar series.

I built a kind of proportional measuring device based on a special pair of dividers which a friend, Roger McHugh, had made many years ago. His elegant model is shown in Fig 1.61 above. Exercise 15 (page 54) describes a construction for a simpler device.

There is a huge amount of literature on the Golden section, or Golden proportion, or Golden ratio or Golden cut.

There is even a magazine, the *Fibonacci Quarterly* from the United States which embraces this territory! And it is something that the students at this time need to become aware of through the fact that it has such a ubiquitous appearance in nature (including in the human being). So what is it? It is a ratio, and a very special ratio. It is also called $\varphi$ *(phi)*.

## Phi, *Fibonacci and the 'Golden cut'* ....

What is $\varphi$? This is the symbol given to this quite special number. As a crude approximation it is 1.6180 to four decimal places. It appears in numerous places in nature, in many more than we can dream of, but it is also claimed to be in many places where it is dubious. An amazing set of relationships that applies to very many things should *not* be assumed to apply to everything!

## *Exact value for* phi, *calculated from its definition*

The definition is crucial. One definition is the number derived when a line is cut at a particular place such that:

> *The ratio of the whole to the larger part is the same as the larger part to the smaller.*

Graphically this can be shown along a line as:

| the whole |
|:---:|

| the smaller part | the larger part |
|:---:|:---:|

And the ratios *graphically* expressed would look like this:

Algebraically the exact ratios can be found for this particular division. If we let 1 unit be the length of smaller part and the larger part be unit $x$ units, then the whole will be $1 + x$ units in length. Or again more graphically:

$$1 + x \text{ units}$$

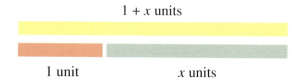

1 unit                    $x$ units

And in conventional mathematical symbolism this is shown as in the pannel opposite and we solve for $x$:

$$\frac{x}{1} = \frac{1+x}{x}$$

## Golden ratio

The Golden ratio or section is $(\sqrt{5} + 1)/2 = 1.618033989...$ as far as most school calculators will go. To calculate this exactly we do the following: Given that we want that the ratio of the whole to the larger is the same as the ratio of the larger to the smaller then we can write

$$\frac{x}{1} = \frac{1+x}{x}$$

Firstly cross multiply: $x^2 = 1 + x$

Rearrange and equate to zero: $x^2 - x - 1 = 0$

This is now a quadratic equation and it can be solved with the formula for $x$ as the unknown (not proved for the students until much later):

$$x = \frac{-b \pm \sqrt{b^2 - 4ac}}{2a}$$

where: $ax^2 + bx + c = 0$

and in this case $a = 1$, $b = -1$ and $c = -1$. Hence, substituting for $a$, $b$ and $c$ we get:

$$x = \frac{-(-1) \pm \sqrt{(-1)^2 - 4 \times 1 \times -1}}{2 \times 1}$$

Simplifying gives: $x = \frac{1 \pm \sqrt{1+4}}{2}$

Or: $x = \frac{1 \pm \sqrt{5}}{2}$

So $x$ is: $x = \frac{1 + \sqrt{5}}{2}$ or $x = \frac{1 - \sqrt{5}}{2}$ exactly.

Yes, that's right, *two* answers. We take the *positive* value only, rewriting it as:

$$x = \frac{\sqrt{5} + 1}{2}$$

The result from the pannel gives us the usual *exact* value for $\varphi$. *T*hus we can write:

$$\varphi = \frac{\sqrt{5}+1}{2}$$

And this, as a non repeating decimal is:

$$\varphi = 1.61803398874989484820458683436564$$

and which is usually remembered as:

$$\varphi = 1.618$$

The negative value $(1-\sqrt{5})/2$ gives the reciprocal $-0.618$. As the number is a ratio, it is immaterial whether expressed as positive or negative.

## *1.618 or 0.618?*

This is the number usually designated as $\varphi$ or *phi*. Sometimes its *reciprocal* is also named *phi*. This is somewhat confusing! But most writers seem to use the value 1.618 (Livio 2002, 80; Critchlow 1969, 30; *www.ams.org*, 2004) rather than 0.618 (Ghyka 1946, 7). Some various references are shown below.

### *Exercise 15   Making a set of Golden section dividers*

A simple set of such dividers can be made from card and pins. The basic structure is straightforward. Suitable model dimensions are shown in Fig 1.62.

1. Draw the four card profiles shown (or design your own, or let the students design them).

2. Score along the red dotted lines (this has the effect of stiffening the dividers arms if bent along the dots).

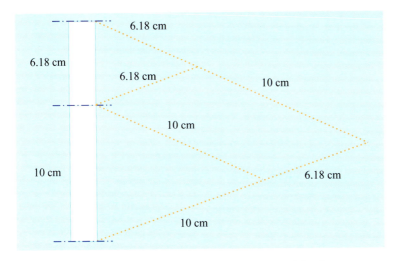

*Fig 1.62  Typical dimensions for a Golden section set of dividers*

3. Pierce holes at the points marked.

4. Cut out the four profiles shown in heavy black outline.

5. Assemble with split pins as pivots.

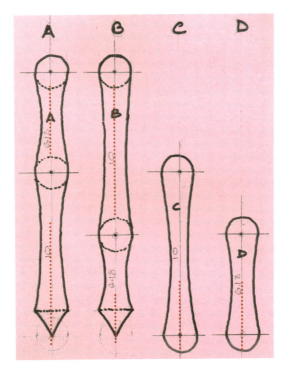

*Fig 1.63*

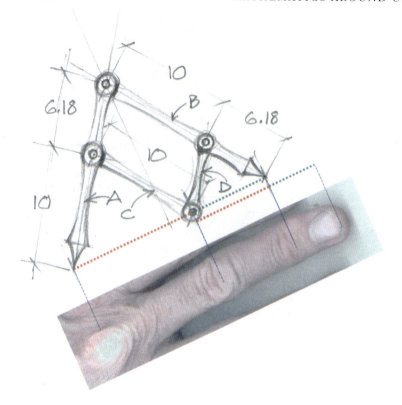

*Fig 1.64 Dividers in use*

6. Check how accurate your dividers are on a ruled measure (10 cm with the wider dividers should give about 6.2 cm with the closer distance)

We can, for instance, check the proportions of the joints of our fingers. See how close these are to this Golden section. If we could see the actual bone joints perhaps it would be more accurate?

Where do we see such proportions in the human head? Is 'MAN' the measure of all things perhaps? Or is this just a mere coincidence? Such is not my conviction.

## *Exercise 16    Golden ratio in the human form*

The students should measure these heights, *A,* and *B,* for themselves to see how close *they* are to this Golden ratio.

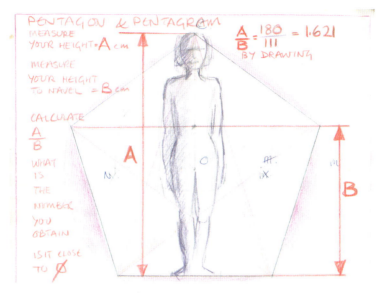

Fig 1.65 *Human proportions*

The young person of this age, not having matured fully, will be somewhat different. See if the group can decide for a greater *or* smaller ratio than $\varphi$ — and *why*.

1. Measure overall height. Let this be *A*.

2. Measure distance to navel from the ground. Let this be *B*

3. Divide *A* by *B*.

4. Make a table of these values.

| *A* | *B* | *A / B* |
|---|---|---|
|  |  |  |
|  |  |  |
|  |  |  |
|  |  |  |
|  |  |  |
|  |  |  |

Fig 1.66 *Table of values*

5. Calculate the average of these ratios. What number is this close to?

The French architect, Le Corbusier, attempted to design a scale which he called the 'Modulor,' based on this proportion, as an aid to design in building. A sketch of this is shown in Fig 1.67.

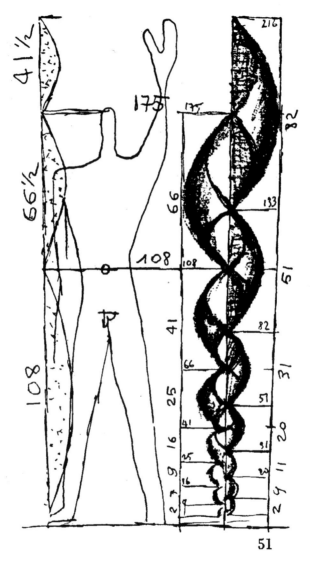

*Fig 1.67 Modulor, a Golden ratio scale (from Le Corbusier, 1954, 51)*

The principal dimensions are 108 and 66.5 in the drawing. If these are added and then divided by 108 we get 1.616, which is close to $\varphi$.

*Exercise 17   Fibonacci in the plant*

Some plants show this Fibonacci series in how they branch. The sneezewort (*Achillea ptarmica*), a type of yarrow, displays this number series in the plane, according to Huntley, as it develops towards its flower heads (Huntley 1970, 163).

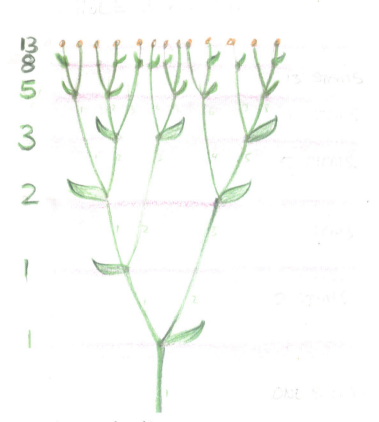

*Fig 1.68  Sneezewort branching*

Note how the leaf nodes appear to line up in this sketch. Does Fennel do something similar? One would have to find some and look! Now that would be an exercise.

*Exercise 18   Phi — The Golden section*

As seen earlier, if we look carefully, there is this particular number which is gradually approached if we take consecutive

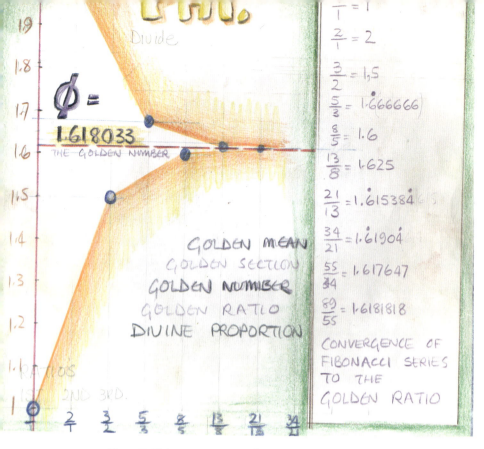

Fig 1.69  Phi, *as a converging limit*

numbers of the Fibonacci series, that is by dividing the latter by the former — for example 5/3 = 1.6666... , and 8/5 = 1.6, and 13/8 = 1.625, etc. These quotients alternate *about* this number but get slowly closer to it — see Fig 1.69.

*Exercise 19   Collage of natures forms*

To conclude the main lesson it may be a good idea to get the students to make a collage of some kind, bringing together drawings, photographs or actual artifacts that exhibit these simple forms — be they galaxies, operculums, pineapples, hen's eggs, tornadoes, seashells, flower buds or a legion of forms their own observation will discover. Some suggestions are in Fig 1.70 and Fig 1.71.

I always hope that students (and adults!) will slowly begin to see where there is some kind of pattern in nature. If there is a pattern then there is sure to be some maths and geometry. Even at this young age the eye can be open to form.

▲ *Fig 1.70  Spiral shapes*          ▼ *Fig 1.71  Eggs, urns, bud and tree forms …*

# 2. Pythagoras and Numbers

This is a main lesson we have often done with this age group of around 12 to 13 (Year 7). It introduces qualities, kinds and notions of *number* in particular. There is always a relation between number and geometry but here number is emphasized whereas in the 'Maths in Nature' section geometry was emphasized.

## *Why Pythagoras?*

We owe a debt to this time of Ancient Greece, for the individuality of Pythagoras must have been one of many who took such a searching stance towards knowledge that most of us can still be challenged by it and are far from emulating it.

These great individuals saw the whole as a whole, and could also see some of what made it a whole. This was what gave it the order it had. And this was *number.* In the concordance and harmony that spoke through music Pythagoras sought to see how this met the human soul and the way it could lead its life. It is said that in his school, it was music that led the community into the day with special harmonies. Students need to know of his life.

Perhaps that is what these greats were sent for. Thales (*c.* 625–547 BC), Euclid (dates uncertain but *c.* 300–260 BC), Archimedes (*c.* 287–212 BC) and Plato (*c.* 428–348 BC) were among them. And their work lived for around two thousand years before a new approach emerged with the Renaissance in Europe, prepared with the earlier help of Arab scholars. We have to thank much that came from the Arab world for translations and developments which later provided material debate among Renaissance thinkers.

With the students of this age we are at a time when there appears to be a seeking in the young person that asks for a correspondence between what is '*in* the head' and what is *out*side. This is a reflection of what we as humanity went through, and

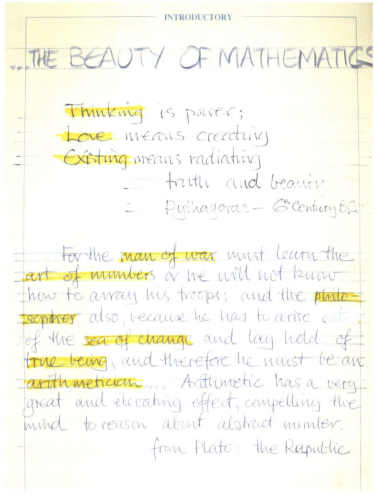

Fig 2.1  *Introductory themes ...*

are still going through historically, with the empiricist and rationalist dichotomy that emerged starkly. It is not so much the dichotomy that is important but the resolution of it. We would not ask a single question if we did not need a resolution of it!

This double-sidedness emerges in this questioning we have. If the inner and outer correspondences were immediately apparent there would be no questioning. But there is. So they are not. And at one age or another this becomes apparent to the young person. We bring a way to meet this emerging problem in such a main lesson as this.

## *Number*

The two aspects concentrated on in our Year 7 main lessons are number and geometry. *Geometry* was covered in the previous main lesson and *number* is studied in this main lesson of about three weeks. Needless to say these two directions overlap but here there is an emphasis on number relations of all sorts. And in particular this is the history of number and number systems. Why number? Is it that in this world we quickly start to see some order, some patterns?

Not all cultures were obsessed with the number ten, and thus the decimal system, as we are almost universally today. We could of course put this down to the fact of ten fingers, but the ancients in Chaldea had sixty in mind — one has to wonder why.

Or there is *one, two* and *many,* which we could accuse the so-called primitives of working with. One aboriginal group counted with a sort of trinitarian base (Fig 2.3). Here the new repeating step began after three steps, not ten.

Yet there are mysteries in numbers, they are not merely a scheme for counting out the dollars, bums on seats, number puzzles, even the current Sudoku craze, or how high a high-rise measures. There is music here — as well as counting and measuring.

*Fig 2.2  A handy start to counting*

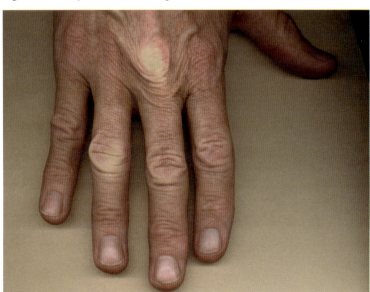

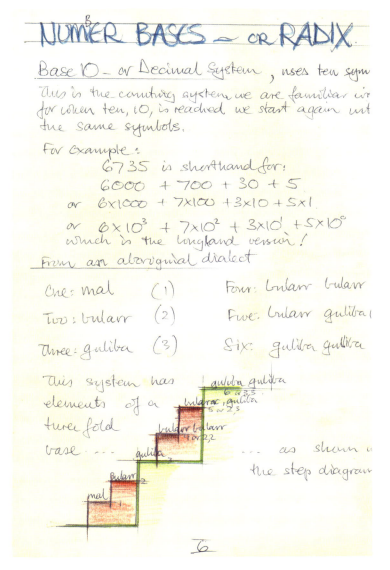

## NUMBER BASES — OR RADIX.

Base 10 — or Decimal System, uses ten symb...

This is the counting system we are familiar wi...
for when ten, 10, is reached we start again wi...
the same symbols.

For example:

6735 is shorthand for:

6000 + 700 + 30 + 5

or 6×1000 + 7×100 + 3×10 + 5×1.

or 6×10³ + 7×10² + 3×10¹ + 5×10⁰
which is the longhand version!

From an aboriginal dialect

One: mal        (1)        Four: bular bular

Two: bular      (2)        Five: bular guliba(

Three: guliba   (3)        Six: guliba guliba

This system has
elements of a
three fold
base ... 
... as shown i...
the step diagram

Fig 2.3  An aboriginal dialect — with a threefold base

## Qualitative number

Number in the abstract is our most common usage. It can be reduced to mere *calculation*. How much money is in the bank for instance — as one lady said to me recently when we talked about maths! But number can be viewed quite differently.

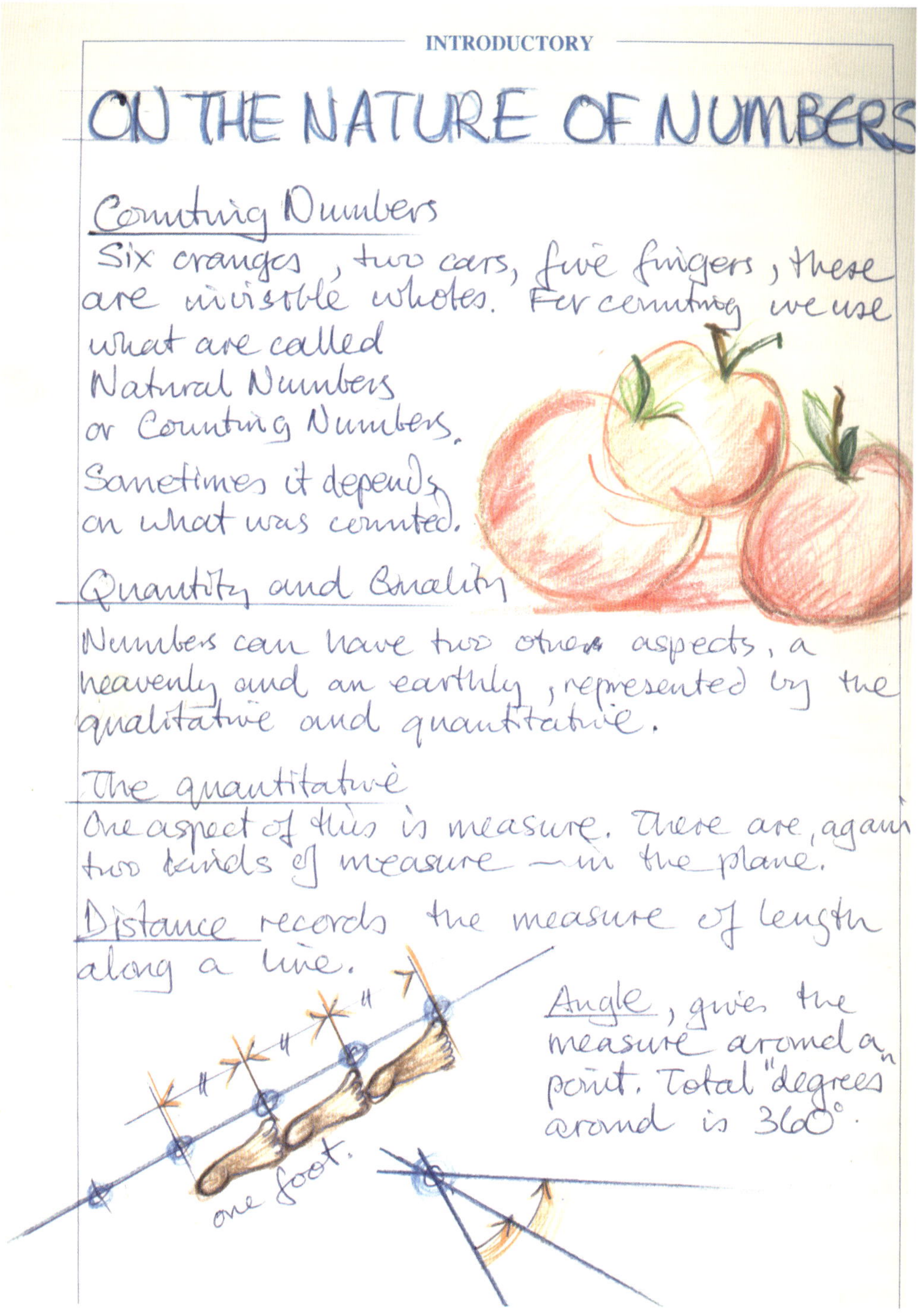
INTRODUCTORY
ON THE NATURE OF NUMBERS
Counting Numbers
Six oranges, two cars, five fingers, these are indivisible wholes. For counting we use what are called
Natural Numbers
or Counting Numbers.
Sometimes it depends on what was counted.
Quantity and Quality
Numbers can have two other aspects, a heavenly and an earthly, represented by the qualitative and quantitative.
The quantitative
One aspect of this is measure. There are, again two kinds of measure — in the plane.
Distance records the measure of length along a line.
Angle, gives the measure around a point. Total "degrees" around is 360°.
one foot.

*Fig 2.4 The qualitative and the quantitative*

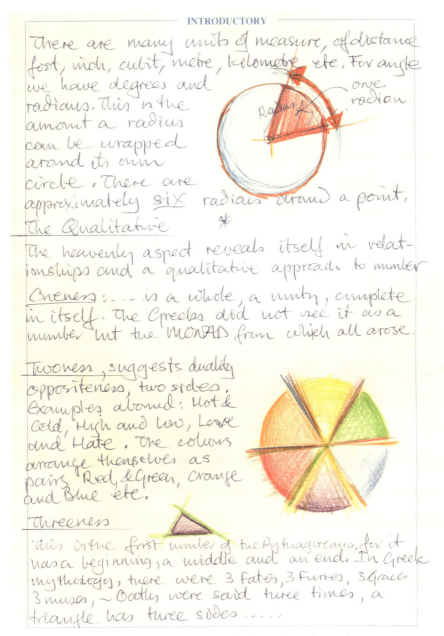

INTRODUCTORY

There are many units of measure, of distance foot, inch, cubit, metre, kilometre etc. For angle we have degrees and radians. This is the amount a radius can be wrapped around its own circle. There are approximately six radians around a point.

one radian

The Qualitative *

The heavenly aspect reveals itself in relationships and a qualitative approach to number

Oneness: ..... is a whole, a unity, complete in itself. The Greeks did not see it as a number but the MONAD from which all arose.

Twoness, suggests duality oppositeness, two sides. Examples abound: Hot & Cold, High and Low, Love and Hate. The colours arrange themselves as pairs Red, & Green, Orange and Blue etc.

Threeness

this is the first number of the Pythagoreans, for it has a beginning, a middle and an end. In Greek mythology, there were 3 Fates, 3 Furies, 3 Graces 3 muses, ~ Oaths were said three times, a triangle has three sides .....

*Fig 2.5  The heavenly or the qualitative*

Is there something about unity that is essentially *different* from a twoness or duality, or a threefoldness (trinities), sevens or fives or even tens? There is far, far more to it than *the One* and *the Many!*

*Exercise 20*

Explore qualities of the numbers up to at least twelve (say). What can we say about 'one-ness' for instance? Is all one? What about the bits? And so on ... much could be debated.

1. Consider unity.

2. Two. Two-ness. Duality. Dichotomies. Look for opposites. This is where one thing is qualitatively different from another, for instance hot and cold, up and down, plane and point. List at least three more such opposites or dualities.

3. Trinities, can we find any? A fundamental trinity is that in geometry, with the three-some which are the very elements of geometry — that is *point, line* and *plane.* I do not believe it is good enough to say, as Keith Critchlow appears to, that one derives from the other (Critchlow 1976, 10–13) as they are mutually *interdependent* (see Fig 2.6). And are totally different in kind. Are RED, BLUE and YELLOW to be considered a trinity? Most of us will talk of them as the *three* primary colors. Find three more trinities. Dimensions in space ...

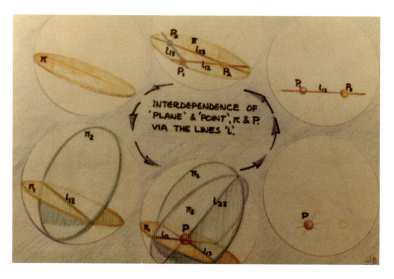

*Fig 2.6 Mutually defining point line and plane. E.g. Three points define a plane. Three planes define a point.*

4. Where do we see the fourfold? Heart beats per breath? Kingdoms of nature?

    Can we find more. Note that when considering the four kingdoms that, although we may say 'four,' each one of them is radically different to another — there is a serious qualitative difference.

5. Where do we see the fivefold? Check out the Rosaceae.

6. Where do we see the sixfold? Check out the Liliacea. some insects — why, one wonders, just *that* many legs? Something to do with three times twofold?

7. Where do we see sevenfoldness?

8. Any 'eights' around? Arachnids.

9. Nines? Christian Hierarchies, rods around a central axis forming the centrioles in cells.

10. Here we can get toey ...

11. This is a hard one ........

12. Dozens?

13. Challenge — to find 'thirteens.'

14. What is essential about 'a hundred'

15. Any other numbers with special qualities?

## Various number systems

Number systems throughout the world have been based on a range of blocks of numbers. From the method of counting in units, to pairs (blocks of two), to threes as mentioned above, to packages of six, to ten (fingers), to twelve (duo-decimal) to twenty and even sixty. And there were many different ways. The

Roman way was different to the Arabic or Hindu way. There have been all kinds of different symbols for each of the numbers. The ancient Egyptians used a base ten — the symbols being as represented in Fig 2.7.

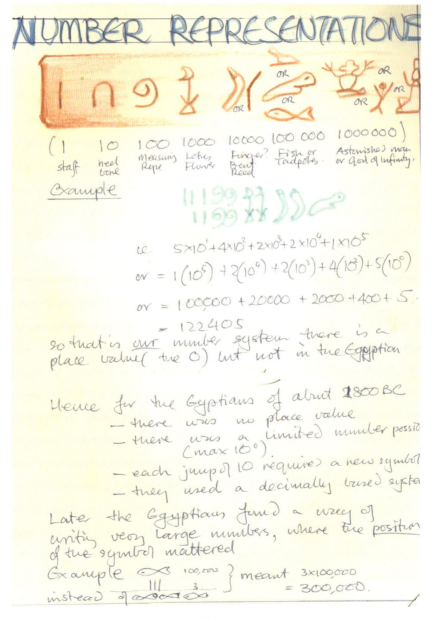

Fig 2.7 Egyptian symbols used to give our number 122405

## *Decimal numbers, whole index form (longhand) and our normal shorthand form*

All of us are familiar with the system of tens. This derives its strength from the notion of place and the inclusion of *nothing, no-thing* or zero. This is called the *base ten* system.

If I write down the number 1 then this is far from 10, which is a lot more than 1 with absolutely *nothing* after it. The fact of putting the zero to the right means that the 1 implies, in this case, *ten* more such ones. So our number depends upon the *place* we put it. To add to the fun we also have different *symbols* for the *number* of 1's we have.

It was the genius of the Hindu and Arab world of yesteryear to give the series of symbols which developed into those we use today. These symbols could have been any kind of glyph but we have ended up with ten of them, if we include the mysterious zero.

These symbols are:

| Symbol | Meaning of symbol |
|---|---|
| 0 | Nothing |
| 1 | 1 |
| 2 | 1 + 1 |
| 3 | 1 + 1 + 1 |
| 4 | 1 + 1 + 1 + 1 |
| 5 | 1 + 1 + 1 + 1 + 1 |
| 6 | 1 + 1 + 1 + 1 + 1 + 1 |
| 7 | 1 + 1 + 1 + 1 + 1 + 1 + 1 |
| 8 | 1 + 1 + 1 + 1 + 1 + 1 + 1 + 1 |
| 9 | 1 + 1 + 1 + 1 + 1 + 1 + 1 + 1 + 1 |

It may seem trivial to point this out, but **9** is a seriously significant reduction in writing, in time and in space, compared to **1 + 1 + 1 + 1 + 1 + 1 + 1 + 1 + 1**. But there is more. Far greater economies, simplifications and conveniences occur if we write numbers using this place system as well. Having collapsed **1 + 1 + 1 + 1 + 1 + 1 + 1 + 1** to **9** and not even having reached **10** it is most impressive that we can further collapse large numbers by a further simple device. This is not a symbol as such but a way in which a process is presented.

Recapping all the units ....

1 + 1 + 1 + 1 + 1 + 1 + 1 + 1 + 1 + 1 + 1 + 1 + 1 + 1 + 1 + 1 + 1 + 1 +
1 + 1 + 1 + 1 + 1 + 1 + 1 + 1 + 1 + 1 + 1 + 1 + 1 + 1 + 1 + 1 + 1 + 1 +
1 + 1 + 1 + 1 + 1 + 1 + 1 + 1 + 1 + 1 + 1 + 1 + 1 + 1 + 1 + 1 + 1 + 1 +
1 + 1 + 1 + 1 + 1 + 1 + 1 + 1 + 1 + 1 + 1 + 1 + 1 + 1 + 1 + 1 + 1 + 1 +
1 + 1 + 1 + 1 + 1 + 1 + 1 + 1 + 1 + 1 + 1 + 1 + 1 + 1 + 1 + 1 + 1 + 1

Collecting these in blocks of 10
$= 10 + 10 + 10 + 10 + 10 + 10 + 10 + 10 + 10 + 10$

Multiplying the number *of* blocks *by* the number *in* each block.
$= 10 \times 10$

Which is:
$= 100$

And now if we raise the block to the *power* of the number of blocks, i.e. 2 in this case, we can write $10^2$. This is the ultimate condensation (so to say) used today.
    So we can be extra economical with large numbers.

| 100 | = | $10 \times 10$ | = $10^2$ |
| 1 000 | = | $10 \times 10 \times 10$ | = $10^3$ |
| 10 000 | = | $10 \times 10 \times 10 \times 10$ | = $10^4$ |
| 100 000 | = | $10 \times 10 \times 10 \times 10 \times 10$ | = $10^5$ |

And even *very* large numbers. Would any one like to write out 10 000 000 000 000 000 000 000 000 every time? No! So we write, simply, $10^{25}$ which means, ... well go figure!

## Longhand and shorthand

This method enables even these index or power numbers to be written very simply. If we have the number 76 540 (say) then what this really means is:

the sum of:
 70 000 + 6 000 + 500 + 40

or the sum in multiples of the tens
 7 × 10 000 + 6 × 1000 + 5 × 100 + 4 × 10

which is when written as powers
 $7 \times 10^4 + 6 \times 10^3 + 5 \times 10^2 + 4 \times 10^1$

So the *shorthand* version, 76540
 *means,* in longhand $7 \times 10^4 + 6 \times 10^3 + 5 \times 10^2 + 4 \times 10^1$

*Exercise 21 — Decimals in long and shorthand*

1. Write out 360 in *longhand*
 $3 \times 10^2 + 6 \times 10^1$

2. Write in shorthand  $5 \times 10^4 + 9 \times 10^3 + 1 \times 10^2 + 2 \times 10^1$
 59 120

3. So longhand for 365 is?
 $3 \times 10^2 + 6 \times 10^1 + 5 \times 10^0$

4. What then is
 $5 \times 10^4 + 3 \times 10^3 + 2 \times 10^2 + 9 \times 10^1 + 7 \times 10^0$
 in shorthand?
                         53 297

(Note: we have implied that $10^0 = 1$. To justify this may be a bit much for some Year 7's but if they can get the hang of indices or powers then they could be led through the following:

$$1 = \frac{5}{5} = \frac{5^1}{5^1} = 5^{1-1} = 5^0$$

(This means that if all these equalities *are* equal then $5^0 = 1$. But we could have chosen *any* number, not just 5. Hence we can say that $x^0 = 1$, where $x$ is any number. So that $10^0 = 1$ if $10 = x$. In other words anything to the power zero is one.

Now that means also that $2^0 = 1$ as well. We will need this to continue to deal with binary numbers — in other words, using base 2, rather than 10.

## *Binary numbers*

A modern number system that we find in the calculator and computer is that based on the number two, or *base two* system. The students may not come across this much yet — or will they? Base two is interpreted often as *on* or *off*, two key conditions of any electrical circuit. *Active* or *Inactive*. And these are often represented symbolically as **1** (active) and **0** (inactive).

This figure **1** means *on* and **0** usually means *off*. Sometimes control switches on electrical hardware have markings just so although mostly we see a kind of combination of a **1** and an **O**.

Sometimes we also see numbers of the form **101011**. What does this mean? How big, or small, is this number?

If all these ones and zeros represent the presence or absence of the number two to some power, and place is also important how then do we interpret such numbers? Just as we considered powers of **10** for base **10** numbers, we consider powers of **2** for base two numbers.

It is helpful to make a table of powers of two to start with. The second column becomes familiar with usage.

*Fig 2.8 Machine on / off switch combining
1 and 0 in its marking*

$$2^0 = 1 \qquad\qquad\qquad\qquad\qquad\qquad 1$$
$$2^1 = 2 \qquad\qquad\qquad\qquad\qquad\qquad 2$$
$$2^2 = 2 \times 2 \qquad\qquad\qquad\qquad\qquad 4$$
$$2^3 = 2 \times 2 \times 2 \qquad\qquad\qquad\qquad 8$$
$$2^4 = 2 \times 2 \times 2 \times 2 \qquad\qquad\qquad 16$$
$$2^5 = 2 \times 2 \times 2 \times 2 \times 2 \qquad\qquad 32$$
$$2^6 = 2 \times 2 \times 2 \times 2 \times 2 \times 2 \qquad 64$$
$$2^7 = 2 \times 2 \times 2 \times 2 \times 2 \times 2 \times 2 \qquad 128$$
$$2^8 = 2 \times 2 \times 2 \times 2 \times 2 \times 2 \times 2 \times 2 \qquad 256$$
$$2^9 = 2 \times 2 \times 2 \times 2 \times 2 \times 2 \times 2 \times 2 \times 2 \qquad 512$$

*Exercise 22   Converting binary to base 10*

1. What is the binary number      **1**      **1**            **1**   to base 10?

| | | |
|---|---|---|
| This means | $=$ | $1 \times 2^2 + 1 \times 2^1 + 1 \times 2^0$ |
| or | $=$ | $1 \times 4 \ + 1 \times 2 \ + 1 \times 1$ |
| or | $=$ | $4 \qquad + 2 \qquad + 1$ |
| or that is | $=$ | $7$ |

This is sometimes written as   $111_2 = 7_{10}$

2. Another example. What is      **1**      **0**      **1**      **0**
   to base 10?

| | | |
|---|---|---|
| | $=$ | $1 \times 2^3 + 0 \times 2^2 + 1 \times 2^1 + 0 \times 2^0$ |
| | $=$ | $1 \times 8 \ + 0 \times 4 \ + 1 \times 2 \ + 0 \times 1$ |
| | $=$ | $8 \quad + \ 0 \ + \ 2 \ + \ 0$ |
| | $=$ | $10$ |
| That is | | $1010_2 = 10_{10}.$ |

3. What is **1000**$_2$ converted to base 10?          8

4. What is **101011**$_2$ converted to base 10?  32+0+8+0+2+1 = 49

5. But what about **145**$_{10}$ converted to binary or base 2? (see table above)

First subtract the highest power of 2 less than 145.
That is 145 − 128 = 17.
Now subtract the highest power less than 17.

# BINARY NUMBERS , uses two symbols only

## 'On/Off' Numbers.

Example: What does 100110 represent (indec

Each symbol represents a place for a power of two

| shorthand | 1 | O | O | 1 | 1 | O |
|---|---|---|---|---|---|---|

or as power    $1 \times 2^5 + 0 \times 2^4 + 0 \times 2^3 + 1 \times 2^2 + 1 \times 2^1 + 0 \times 2^0$

or    $32 + 0 + 0 + 4 + 2 + 0$

or    $32 + 4 + 2 = 38$

Hence    $38_{ten} = 100110_{two}$,

## Table

| DEC.x | {POWERS TO GIVE x. | ALL POWERS | BINARY SHORTHAN |
|---|---|---|---|
| 1 | $2^0$ | $2^0 \times 1$ | 1 |
| 2 | $2^1$ | $2^1 \times 1 + 2^0 \times 0$ | 1 0 |
| 3 | $2^1 + 2^0$ | $2^1 \times 1 + 2^0 \times 1$ | 1 1 |
| 4 | $2^2$ | $2^2 \times 1 + 2^1 \times 0 \ 2^0 \times 0$ | 1 0 0 |
| 5 | $2^2 + 2^0$ | $2^2 \times 1 + 2^1 \times 0 \ 2^0 \times 1$ | 1 0 1 |
| 6 | $2^2 + 2^1$ | $2^2 \times 1 + 2^1 \times 1 \ 2^0 \times 0$ | 1 1 0 |
| 7 | $2^2 + 2^1 + 2^0$ | $2^2 \times 1 + 2^1 \times 1 \ 2^0 \times 1$ | 1 1 1 |
| 8 | $2^3$ | $2^3 \times 1 + 2^2 \times 0 + 2^1 \times 0 + 2^0 \times 0$ | 1 0 0 0 |
| 9 | $2^3 + 2^0$ | $2^3 \times 1 + 2^2 \times 0 + 2^1 \times 0 + 2^0 \times 1$ | 1 0 0 1 |
| 10 | $2^3 + 2^1$ | $2^3 \times 1 + 2^2 \times 0 + 2^1 \times 1 \ 2^0 \times 0$ | 1 0 1 0 |

*Fig 2.9  Binary numbers*

That is $17 - 16 = 1$.
Thus we have $145 = 128 + 16 + 1$.
Or, putting in missing powers:

$145 = 1 \times 128 + 0 \times 64 + 0 \times 32 + 1 \times 16 + 0 \times 8 + 0 \times 4 + 0 \times 2 + 1 \times 1$
$145_{10} = 1 \quad\quad 0 \quad\quad 0 \quad\quad 1 \quad\quad 0 \quad\quad 0 \quad\quad 0 \quad\quad 1_2$

6. What is $999_{10}$ in binary?

$512 + 256 + 128 + 64 + 32 + 0 + 0 + 4 + 2 + 1 = 1 1 1 1 1 0 0 1 1 1$

7. And finally show that $38_{10}$ is the same as $100110_2$.

## Measurement

Counting numbers and their systems are one thing but there is
something else to count apart from things, for measurement is
a thing in itself! If we wish to *measure* anything too we have
recourse to number — but also something else. To count distance, for instance, we have to have some standardized measure.
The different standards of measure are legion. Or were. Today
many countries use the metric system, others the imperial (even
the USA). Before that there were many other standards. Before
going too far we need to recognize there are two fundamentally
different kinds of measure in the plane.

## Distance and angle

In our ordinary day-to-day space these two are *distance* and
*angle.* That is distance *along* a line and angle *around* a line (or
point). Imagine how different these are.

In the one case we step along a line in, let us say, equal
lengths. A good measure of such distances would be our length
of pace, or for somewhat shorter, the length of our foot. This is
indeed a measure — the foot — still used in many places.

In early times another measure was used by a number of cultures, the *cubit.* But how long was a cubit? Was this the length of

# UNITS OF MEASURE

Why do we measure? To compare of thing with another — for length, for size, for area for volume and for length of time.

Early in human history artefacts were compared with the human form. The human was the standard. Much later part of the earths surface became the basis for measure (the metre). Later still the wavelength of a coloured light. Babylonian and Egyptian peoples, long ago used the CUBIT, ie the length of the forearm from elbow to finger tips.

The Cubit.

Comparison of Students

Historically: Egypt 52.3 cm  Babylon 49.61 cm.
Assyria 50.37 cm Asia Minor 51.74 cm.

*Fig 2.10  Kinds of measure: the cubit*

Related to the human body are:

Digit —— width of forefinger, 19mm

Hand —— standardised at 4" or 10.2cm.

Span — about 24cm.

Pace — about...

Fathom — now 6'.00 or 183cm

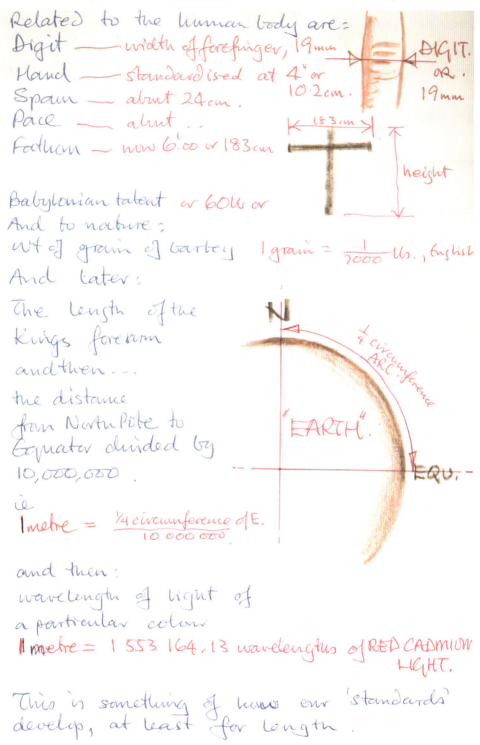

DIGIT. OR. 19mm

183cm

height

Babylonian talent or 60lb or

And to nature:

Wt of grain of barley    1 grain = $\frac{1}{7000}$ lbs., English

And later:

The length of the Kings forearm and then...

the distance from North Pole to Equator divided by 10,000,000.

N

¼ circumference ARC.

"EARTH".

EQU.

ie

$$1 \text{ metre} = \frac{\frac{1}{4} \text{ circumference of E.}}{10\,000\,000}$$

and then:

wavelength of light of a particular colour

1 metre = 1 553 164.13 wavelengths of RED CADMIUM LIGHT.

This is something of how our 'standards' develop, at least for length.

*Fig 2.11  From the King's forearm to wavelengths of light*

the forearm of the Pharaoh or the King? If so, then it inevitably varied. Even among different peoples it varied. For the Egyptians and Babylonians it was about 20 inches or 51 cm (Oxford Junior Encyclopedia 1951, 263). Other sources give other values (see Fig 2.10).

The historical progression of measures seems to have been taken from parts of the highest of the human in the hierarchy (king, etc.), the human form as such, thence to nature (a portion of the Earth's circumference), and, of late, to a certain number of the wavelengths of light.

One quarter the distance from the North Pole to the equator divided by 10 000 000 was deemed in about 1791 by the French Academy of Sciences to be the metre. The epic efforts of Méchain and Delambre resulted in the value of 39.37008 inches for the metre. The word derives from the Greek word that means measure, *metron*. Nowadays there is a reverse definition in that the metre is said to be that distance traveled by light in a vacuum in 1/299 792 458 of a second! (This assumes that light has a 'speed' in the ordinary sense — which is contestable.) This is given in the SI (International System of Units) definition. Most of us are happy to pace something out if we want a reasonable idea of the length of a housing block. But for some purposes much greater accuracy is needed. Especially if you are buying the block!

*Exercise 23   Distance measures*

1. Find a number of *distance* measures and state their estimated lengths in both inches and centimetres in a table.

2. How long is one inch in millimetres?   25.4

3. Find the average cubit length in Fig 2.10 above.   52.255 cm

4. Why might the initial French definition of the metre be questionable?
   It assumes that the Earth is an exact sphere. It is not. It is at least a geoid, pear shaped and tetrahedral all at the same time.

5. What was an 'inch' based on?

   A statute from 1284 gives 'Three grains of barley, dry and round, make an inch; twelve inches make a foot; three feet make an ulna [yard].'

## Angular measure

This is a different world. Now there are far fewer units that appear to be used. I have only discovered three. The three are *degree, radian* and *gon* or *grad.* All are based on the full revolution of a circle. The degree is by far the most common. Radians are more for the mathematical types. And the 'gon' I only came across this year.

| UNIT: | PORTION OF A FULL CIRCLE: |
|---|---|
| Degree | 360 to circle |

*(Each degree is made up of 60 minutes and each minute is of 60 seconds)*

| | |
|---|---|
| Radian | $1/2\pi$ (or about 57 degrees). About 6.28 to circle |

*(We deal with some of the mysteries of $\pi$ later in these notes)*

| | |
|---|---|
| Gon, grad | 400 to circle |

*(Each gon or grad is made up of 100 centesimal minutes and each minute is of 100 centesimal seconds)*

The gon is used by surveyors in some European countries. It is an attempt to decimalize a portion of the circle, namely the right-angle. So there are 100 gons to the right-angle. I was familiar with this as the *grad.* If we examine the school calculator we find a choice of *Deg, Rad* or *Gra,* where Gra implies grad. Check it out on your school calculator.

*Exercise 24   Angular measure*

1. How many degrees in a quarter of a circle?  $360/4 = 90$

2. How many degrees in 100 revolutions?
$$360 \times 100 = 36\ 000$$

3. How many gons in 8.345 cycles around a centre?
$$8.345 \times 400 = 3338$$

4. If $\pi = 3.141592653589793$ radians then how many radians in a full circle?      $3.141592653589793 \times 2 = 6.2831853071796$

5. How do each of these three compare, that is if a degree is *one* unit how big or small is a grad and how big is a radian in degrees
   $1 : ? : ?$
   A grad is $90/100$ degrees $= 0.9$ degrees. A radian is $360 / 2\pi$ degrees $= 59.2957$ degrees. Hence   $1 : 0.9 : 59.2957$

## Familiar measuring instruments

Distance is measured with a straight ruler graduated in centimetres (as well as in inches in some countries) and usually 30 cm long.

Angle is measured with a protractor usually graduated in blocks of ten degrees in 1 degree divisions and takes the form of a semi-circle (less commonly a full circle).

These two instruments indicate two fundamentally different worlds — linear (straight line) and the circular (the curve). The distinctions between the two has significant ramifications later on, as the measures of one are *incommensurable* with the other in whole-number terms. We see this in the circle where for a circle of 2 units diameter the circumference is
$$2 \times \pi = 2 \times 3.141592653589793 \ldots$$
$$= 6.2831853071796 \ldots \text{ units.}$$

This is connected with one of the three famous ancient problems, the one framed as 'squaring the circle,' where it was put out as a challenge to find with compass and ruler how to construct a square equal in its area to a circles area of known radius.

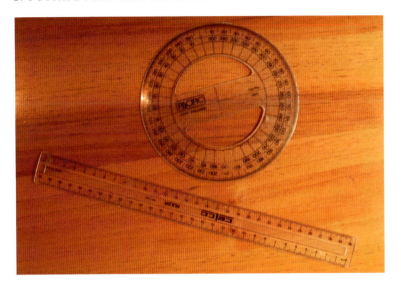

*Fig 2.12  The two basic drawing instruments*

This was in due time proved to be impossible and could not have been solved by the ancients as it requires the length of $\sqrt{\pi}$ 'but classical constructions can only produce algebraic numbers' (Gullberg 1997, 422) and $\pi$ is a transcendental number, not just an irrational.

## Kinds of numbers

The various kinds of numbers are summarized below in Fig 2.13 (so far as the real numbers are concerned.)

## Prime numbers and the sieve of Eratosthenes

There is a whole fascinating range of numbers greater than one for which we can find nothing which will divide into them (except the number itself — and one). These are called the *prime* numbers. If *one* is not considered prime then the first prime is *two*. The next is three. But four is not prime, as it can be divided by 2.

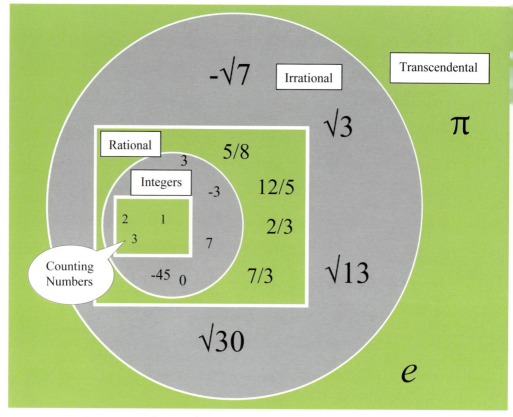

*Fig 2.13 Number sets from counting numbers to transcendental numbers*

They are mysterious as no one can give a definitive predictive law cornerning them: a number can only be checked as to *whether* it is a prime.

How is this done? Simply by finding if it has any factors. What is a factor? Leonardo Fibonacci of Pisa called the primes *incomposite* numbers because if they were composite they were not primes. A factor is a number which divides the supposed prime giving another number with no remainder. For example: 99 is not a prime. It can be divided by 9 giving 11 with no remainder.

But 97 *is* a prime. It will not divide by 2 or 3. Or by 4, 5, 6, 7, 8, 9 or 10 and leave no remainder. Nor will it divide by any number between 11 and 98. Test this. It gets tedious after a while. Imagine trying to check whether 987 654 321 is a prime! There are a few initial rules that can help. Is the number 987 654 322 a prime? No, it is not, as any number ending in an even number

2. PYTHAGORAS AND NUMBERS                                         85

has at least one factor and that is 2. Suddenly we can eliminate a whole swag of numbers — all the evens or *multiples of two*.

So in the sequence:

1, 2, 3, 4, 5, 6, 7, 8, 9, 10, 11, 12, 13, 14, 15, 16, 17, 18, 19 and 20 we note that all the blue numbers are even, multiples of two and that that is half of them. Does this mean that half the numbers all the way to infinity are even and the other half prime? It may seem so, but is not so at all, as some of these will divide by 3. These are shown in green:

1, 2, 3, 4, 5, 6, 7, 8, 9, 10, 11, 12, 13, 14, 15, 16, 17, 18, 19 and 20
And 5, in red:

1, 2, 3, 4, 5, 6, 7, 8, 9, 10, 11, 12, 13, 14, 15, 16, 17, 18, 19 and 20

This could go on and on and would indeed be tedious but all the numbers *left in the black* would be prime. Not surprisingly there is a diagrammatic or pictorial method worked out by a Greek named Eratosthenes (*c.* 276–194 BC). What he devised is called the *Sieve of Eratosthenes* (Gullberg 1997, 77).

## Sieving for primes

After recognizing that 1 is not considered a prime, we shade alternate numbers *after* 2. Then shade every third number *after* 3 if not already shaded (as in Fig 2.14). And every fifth number *after* 5 if not already shaded and so on. And every seventh after 7 etc. ... Note that the numbers remaining *unshaded* are all prime.

| 1 | 2 | 3 | 4 | 5 | 6 | 7 | 8 | 9 | 10 |
|---|---|---|---|---|---|---|---|---|----|
| 11 | 12 | 13 | 14 | 15 | 16 | 17 | 18 | 19 | 20 |
| 21 | 22 | 23 | 24 | 25 | 26 | 27 | 28 | 29 | 30 |
| 31 | 32 | 33 | 34 | 35 | 36 | 37 | 38 | 39 | 40 |
| 41 | 42 | 43 | 44 | 45 | 46 | 47 | 48 | 49 | 50 |

*Fig 2.14  Eratosthenes sieve from 1 to 50*

*Exercise 25*

1. In the table below continue the shading up to 100. This leaves
   primes only.

| 1 | 2 | 3 | 4 | 5 | 6 | 7 | 8 | 9 | 10 |
|---|---|---|---|---|---|---|---|---|----|
| 11 | 12 | 13 | 14 | 15 | 16 | 17 | 18 | 19 | 20 |
| 21 | 22 | 23 | 24 | 25 | 26 | 27 | 28 | 29 | 30 |
| 31 | 32 | 33 | 34 | 35 | 36 | 37 | 38 | 39 | 40 |
| 41 | 42 | 43 | 44 | 45 | 46 | 47 | 48 | 49 | 40 |
| 51 | 52 | 53 | 54 | 55 | 56 | 57 | 58 | 59 | 60 |
| 61 | 62 | 63 | 64 | 65 | 66 | 67 | 68 | 69 | 70 |
| 71 | 72 | 73 | 74 | 75 | 76 | 77 | 78 | 79 | 80 |
| 81 | 82 | 83 | 84 | 85 | 86 | 87 | 88 | 89 | 90 |
| 91 | 92 | 93 | 94 | 95 | 96 | 97 | 98 | 99 |  |

2. List the primes from 2 to 100
   2, 3, 5, 7, 11, 13, 17, 19, 23, 29, 31, 37, 41, 43, 47, 53, 59, 61,
   67, 71, 73, 79, 83, 89, 97

3. How many primes are there from 2 to 100?          25

4. How many *new* colors did you have to use?
   None as 11, 13, 17 have no multiples not already shaded in

5. Can you detect any patterns in the array of primes?
   Primes sometimes come in pairs of numbers with one between.
   All prime numbers are one more or one less than a number
   divisible by six.

6. Is $1000011_2$ a prime number? (Note: Primeness is independent of base)

$1000011_2 = 1 \times 64 + 0 \times 32 + 0 \times 16 + 0 \times 8 + 0 \times 4 + 1 \times 2 + 1 \times 1 = 2^6 + 2^1 + 2^0 = 67_{10}$ . Yes.

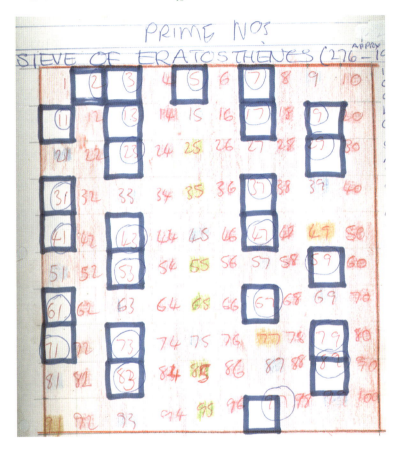

*Fig 2.15  Sieve of Eratosthenes — another presentation*

## Pythagorean Triads

What is the number relationship that Pythagoras himself is so well known for?

### Exercise 26   Pythagorean Triads

This is an exercise to explore what we call 'Pythagorean Triads.' What two whole numbers, which, when their squares

are added, will lead to a further *whole* number that is itself
a whole number *squared?* (We note that four squared, or $4^2$,
means $4 \times 4$.)

Do the following two numbers fit this requirement?

1. 40 and 30? Yes, as $30^2$ added to $40^2$, or $(30 \times 30) + (40 \times 40)$,
   gives 2500. And 2500 is of course $50^2$, that is 50 is the *square
   root* of 2500. Now test these.

2. 20 and 30?

3. 3 and 4

4. 5 and 13

5. 12 and 5

6. 1 and 1

7. 240 and 250

Is there a rule that we can find that will tell us how we can set up
such a *Pythagorean Triad* — that is not trial and error?

Yes there is, and it is not too difficult and this is elaborated in
the next exercise (Exercise 27). But not from all and any numbers that we try, will we get two numbers that will give a *perfect
square.*

If, however, our whole number is not a perfect square *can* we
find this square root? There is an *algorithm* (or method) and it is
calculator free, but more later on this.

Meanwhile how do we form such triads?

*Exercise 27  Pythagorean Triads, a method to determine them*

For the three pro-numerals (i.e., letters representing some
unknowns), *a, b* and *c* we let
$a^2 + b^2 = c^2$

Now we let      $a = 2pq, \quad b = p^2 - q^2 \quad$ and $\quad c = p^2 + q^2$

where $p$ and $q$ are both positive integers (i.e. positive whole numbers), also where $p$ is *greater* than $q$ (or, symbolically, $p > q > 0$).

With these provisos we can construct some *triads*. Try the following:

1. Let $p = 4$ and $q = 3$ (they are both positive integers, i.e. $4 > 3$, and $p$ is even, but $q$ is not. What are $a$, $b$ and $c$?

So $a = 2 \times 4 \times 3 = 24$, $b = 4^2 - 3^2 = 7$ and $c = 4^2 + 3^2 = 25$

(Check that:  $a^2 + b^2 = c^2$
then substituting $24^2 + 7^2 = 24 \times 24 + 7 \times 7$ where $a = 24$ and $b = 7$
and so                                     $= 576 + 49$
and                                        $= 625$
hence                                      $= 25^2$, and this is $c$ squared as expected)

Now try these ......

2. Let $p = 2$ and $q = 1$  (this is a favorite!)   What are $a$, $b$ and $c$?

3. Let $p = 3$ and $q = 2$  What are $a$, $b$ and $c$?

4. Let $p = 5$ and $q = 2$  What are $a$, $b$ and $c$?

5. Let $p = 4$ and $q = 2$ What are $a$, $b$ and $c$?

6. List the first four Pythagorean Triads.


Are there other conditions which need to be imposed on $p$ and $q$? Books say that one number, but not both, must be even (i.e. divisible by two). Is this so?

The above method can find the 'pure' triads so to say. But it is still possible to find a value for $c$ without specials conditions. We can see this graphically (or geometrically) with a further exercise. But first a little exploration with some diagrams.

The answer to No. 2 above was $a = 4$, $b = 3$ and $c = 5$. What does it mean in *space* (or rather the plane) to say that the sum of the square of a number and another different number is equal to the square of a third number (Fig 2.16)?

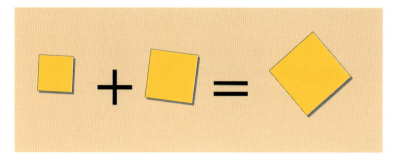

*Fig 2.16  Adding squares?*

Can this be arranged a little more meaningfully? Sure can. We find we can place these squares together to form a triangle *in space* (Fig 2.17). It is a most interesting triangle too. For it has three angles (which, as we know, add to 180°) and one of them is a right angle, or 90° (Fig 2.18). There is a mysterious relationship here between number and geometry ... discovered long ago, it seems, in Sumeria, and credited to Pythagoras.

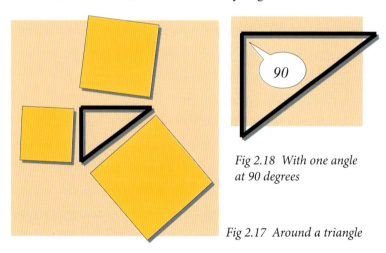

*Fig 2.18  With one angle at 90 degrees*

*Fig 2.17  Around a triangle*

Much more could be said about squares and right angle triangles but for the moment let us draw the *longest* side of a right-angle triangle of unit height and see where this leads.

*Exercise 28   Finding the longest third side of a specific right-angle triangle*

Starting with *unit* side lengths (i.e. side lengths of *one* unit), for a right-angle triangle how do we find the third side? We can, of course, draw it, and this will give us an answer.

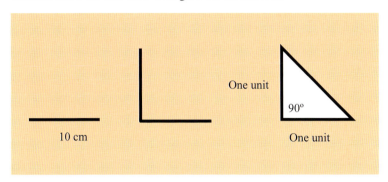

*Fig 2.19*

1. Draw it. That is mark, as a base, a horizontal line 10 cm long (say). We let the unit side be 10 cm long for convenience.

2. Now draw a vertical line from the left-hand end up vertically 10 cm (recall that the construction in Exercise 1 can be used).

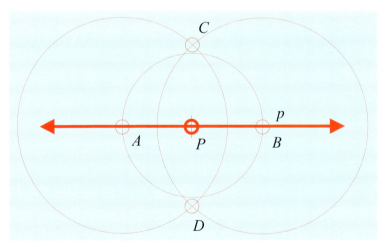

*Fig 2.20*

3. Measure the longest length as accurately as you can. It should be about 14 cm. Or perhaps 14.1 cm. Check. Can we get more accurate still? Is it 14.14 cm maybe? Who would dare to say we can measure to 14.142 cm?

From our numbers we are saying that, as the triangle is right-angled the sum of the squares on the two shorter sides is the same as the square on the longest, the so-called *hypotenuse*.

Now $1^2 + 1^2 = 2$, OK so far.

Or for us here $10^2 + 10^2 = 200$.

But what number *squared* is 2, or, for us, what number squared is 200? Is it 14, or 14.1, or 14.14 or even 14.142? Check the squares of these numbers.

$14 \times 14 = 196$.

$14.1 \times 14.1 = 198.81$. Not too far from 200. And

$14.14 \times 14.14 = 199.9396$. Even closer to 200. And finally (if we *could* measure this accurately) $14.142 \times 14.142 = 199.996164$ which is very much closer to 200.

It could be an interesting exercise in both accuracy of measurement and percentages to see how accurate our actual measures were. So ....

*Exercise 29   What is the square root of 200?*

The students should try to measure first to *no* decimal places (or nearest cm) on their standard centimetre ruler, then to *one* decimal place (i.e. to nearest millimetre) and then to *two* decimal places (at best an estimate to 1/10 of a millimetre). To try to go further with a standard ruler makes little sense as the distances were most likely drawn in the first place with said ruler! Now make a table. As practice complete the table below.

*Fig 2.21*

| Measurements in centimetres | Square this measurement | Subtract from 200 | Divide answer by 200 | and multiply by 100 to give % error |
|---|---|---|---|---|
| 14 | $14 \times 14 = 196$ | $200 - 196 = 4$ | $4/200 = 0.02$ | $0.02 \times 100 = \textbf{2\%}$ |
| 14.1 | | | | |
| 14.14 | | | | $= \textbf{0.0302\%}$ |

What do we notice about the accuracy? Does it get better with more decimal places?

It should of course — but will we ever get to exactly 200? I think not. So the students can begin to see we may have some funny numbers here, numbers for which we cannot get an exact square root.

We cannot actually answer what the square root of 200 is but we do know it is *about* 14.14.

The best of the above is 14.14 and even this gives an error of 0.0151%. Which is not bad. But not *exact* either. This simple little 10 by 10 by 14.14 triangle gave the Greek world a lot of trouble, it is said. For here was a triangle which had no *whole* number for one of its lengths, and was not the world constructed from number?

A further exercise can readily find the first few of these funny numbers. These particular funny numbers are called *surds*, (not *absurds*) or *irrational* numbers. The point is that we have found numbers which are not simple counting numbers. And all because of a few triangles, as the following exercise demonstrates.

## Exercise 30   *The first few surds*

Initially make a ten times scale drawing — this is for the sake of accuracy.

1. Mark a point *O* and draw a line to the left 10 cm long to a point *A*.

2. From *A* draw a perpendicular upwards 10 cm to *B*.

3. Join *OB* forming the triangle *OAB*.

4. Measure *OB* and make this the radius of a circle.

5. Draw an arc from *B* down to the line *OA* finding point *C*. *OC* will be about 14.14 cm (or √200)

6. Draw a further perpendicular up from *C* of 10 cm length to *D*.

7. Join *OD* forming triangle *OCD*.

8. Measure *OD* and make this the radius of another circle.

9. Draw an arc from *D* down to the line *OA* finding point *E. OC* will be about 17.32 cm (or √300)

10. This whole process can be continued indefinitely! But the students should try to get to the next whole number in the sequence. (This will be 3 of course) This is also a good test for accuracy of drawing and compass work.

11. Write in all the radii along the line *OA*. These should be about 10 cm at *A,* 14.14 cm at *C,* 17.32 cm at *E,* 20 cm etc, etc (underneath there are written here only the multiples of the unit values e.g. 1, √2, √3, 2, √5, etc.)

Here we have generated quite a few of these funny numbers. Numbers like 1, 2, 3, 4 and 5 are whole numbers (or integers), while such as √2, √3 and √5 are what we call surds or irrational numbers.

*Fig 2.22*

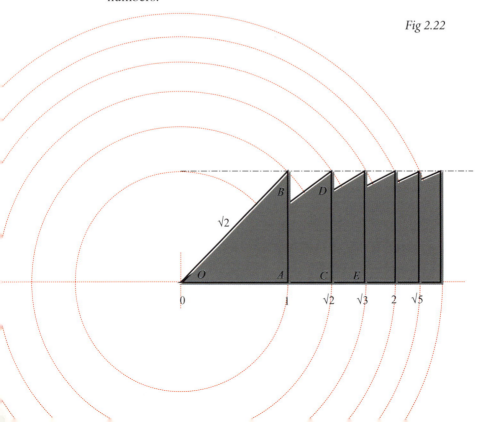

Given that we now have a kind of number which can only be expressed *exactly* using the surd symbol ( √ ) how can we get a good approximation to this — even if not precisely — and without a calculator? For we would not find it helpful to give surds to a manufacturer or carpenter! There is a method (or algorithm) to find a square root. It is a little complicated but not too hard. The first number tested will be a number to which we can work out the answer, simply by ensuring we already know it. For example if we multiply 678 × 678 and get 459 684, then we know that √459 684 is 678. The method is demonstrated in the next exercise. It is a little like a special long division.

## Exercise 31   *Using an algorithm to find a square root*

1. Write out the number (459 684 in this case) in a grid similar to that shown. Draw verticals down every *two* numbers to the left of where the decimal point would be. Ask what number *multiplied by itself* will be closest to but not greater than, 45 (in this case). This will be 6 times 6. Place a 6 above the 5 in the fifth column as shown. Now subtract the 36 from 45 and get the remainder of 9

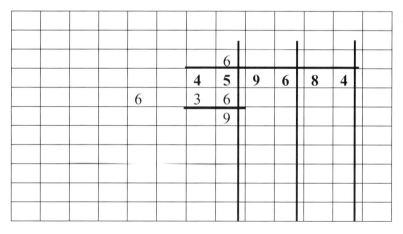

*Fig 2.23*

2. Now take the 6 in the very top row and *double* it. This makes 12. Place the 12 in the 3rd and 4th columns as shown. Now bring down the next two numbers, that is, 96 and place as seen in the sixth row. Now ask what number do we put above the six in

the 10th column which when added to 120 and then multiplied together will be less than 996. It will be 7, as $127 \times 7 = 889$. Place 7 above the 6 in the top row, and place 889 under 996 and subtract giving 107.

*Fig 2.24*

|   |   |   |   |   |   |   |   | 6 |   | 7 |   |
|---|---|---|---|---|---|---|---|---|---|---|---|
|   |   |   |   |   |   | 4 | 5 | 9 | 6 | 8 | 4 |
|   |   |   |   |   | 6 | 3 | 6 |   |   |   |   |
|   |   |   |   |   |   |   |   | 9 | 9 | 6 |   |
|   |   |   | 1 | 2 | 7 |   |   | 8 | 8 | 9 |   |
|   |   |   |   |   |   |   |   | 1 | 0 | 7 |   |

3. Repeat this process. Now take the 67 in the very top row and *double* it. That gives 134. Place the 134 in the second, third and forth columns as shown. Now bring down the next two numbers, that is, 84 and place as seen in the eighth row. Now ask what number do we put above the four in the twelfth column which when added to 1340 and then multiplied together will be less than or equal to 10784. It will be 8, as $1348 \times 8 = 10784$. Place 10784 under 10784 and subtract giving exactly **zero**.

*Fig 2.25*

|   |   |   |   |   |   |   | 6 |   | 7 |   | 8 |   |
|---|---|---|---|---|---|---|---|---|---|---|---|---|
|   |   |   |   |   |   | 4 | 5 | 9 | 6 | 8 | 4 |   |
|   |   |   |   |   | 6 | 3 | 6 |   |   |   |   |   |
|   |   |   |   |   |   |   | 9 | 9 | 6 |   |   |   |
|   |   |   | 1 | 2 | 7 |   | 8 | 8 | 9 |   |   |   |
|   |   |   |   |   |   |   | 1 | 0 | 7 | 8 | 4 |   |
|   | 1 | 3 | 4 | 8 |   |   | 1 | 0 | 7 | 8 | 4 |   |
|   |   |   |   |   |   |   |   |   |   |   | 0 |   |

Since there is no remainder we can assert that the square root of 459684 is exactly 678. *Why* this method works is another matter.

But suppose we do not have a nice whole number with an exact square root? This method can neverless discover it. Ask the class to find the square root of 2 to *ten* decimal places. Most school calculators will only go to nine decimal places so to demand ten poses a wee problem! But no — we have the above algorithm. If I recall rightly I did do this once with a Year 7 group. They can be led through the process.

## Exercise 32   *The square root of any number (in particular √2)*

1. Find the square root of 2 to ten decimal places. Ouch! We start exactly as above, with placing the 2 in front of a decimal point but this time putting 22 (yes) zeros after the decimal point.

*Fig 2.26*

2. Now we ask what number times itself will go into 2, answer 1 × 1 = 1. So place the 1 above the 2 and place a 1 in line with the row below the 2 and also place the multiple of 1 × 1 = 1 immediately under the 2 as well.

*Fig 2.27*

3. Now subtract the 1 from the 2. This gives 1 again. Now bring down two zeros making 100. Place *double* the very top 1 on the left-hand side and multiply by 10 making 20.

   Now test for a number less than 100 from 22 × 2 = 44, 23 × 3 = 69, and 24 × 4 = 96. Only 24 and 4 gives a number with a remainder less than 24 when subtracted from 100. This is a good exercise in *estimating*.

*Fig 2.28*

4. Subtract 96 from 100, this leaves a remainder of 4. Now again bring down two zeros making 400. Continue this whole process.

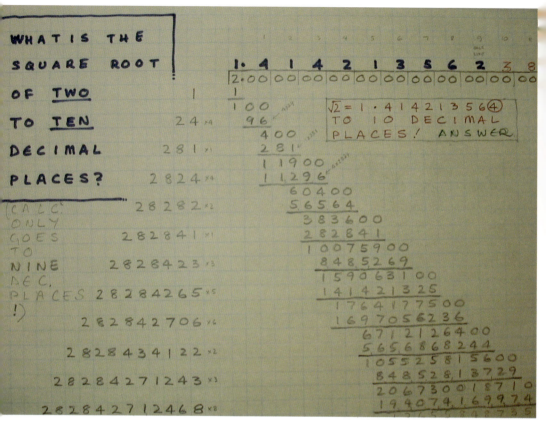

*Fig 2.29 Calculation for the square root of two*

The result up to 11 decimal places is shown here (why eleven and not just ten?).

This is an excellent exercise in numerical accuracy and the processes involved are addition, subtraction, multiplication and estimating. It is easy to make a mistake, although a check with the calculator can keep us on the right track until the last minute, or rather, last two decimal places required.

*Exercise 33   Square roots (but no calculator please)*

1. Find the square root of 1 522 756 exactly.     1234

2. Find the square root of 2.618 to two decimal places.     1.62

3. Find the square root of three to three decimal places.     1.732

4. Find the square root of 3 to *ten* decimal places (over the weekend!)
   1.732 050 807 568 9...... which rounds off to 1.732 050 807 6 to
   ten places

5. Can you find the square root of –1 (is this even *possible?*)
   No

## Pythagoras theorem

This is usually stated as:

> For a right-angle triangle, the square on
> the hypotenuse is equal to the sum of the
> squares on the other two sides.

As can be seen there are many right-angle triangles for which
we do not need fancy ways, or even a calculator, to find a
square root. This is when we already know what the square of
a number is.

Some examples of such familiar triads are:

3 – 4 – 5,  5 – 12 – 13,  7 – 24 – 25,

and multiples of these such as 6 – 8 – 10,  21 – 72 – 75.

We also saw how we can find a good approximation to the
square root of a number if there is no whole number solution.

This is all well and good. But mathematician types need to
know things for certain, for all cases and forever! Which is why
they make such a fuss about *proofs*. To show a few special cases
can be called *demonstration* but it is not proof. So we appeal to
the exigencies of logic. We trust our thinking.

Algebraic proofs belong to later years so only some of those
that involve constructions will be shown here.

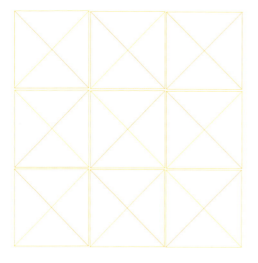

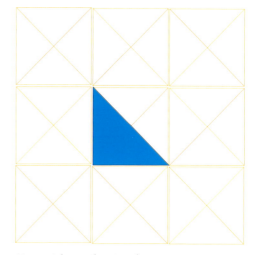

*For a right-angle triangle ...*

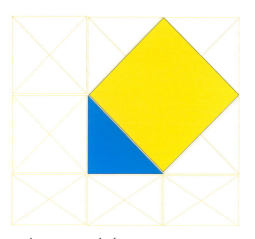

*... the square on the hypotenuse ...*

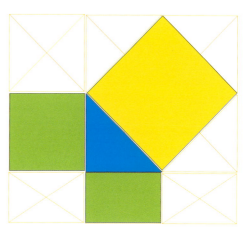

*... is equal to the sum of the squares on the other two sides*

*Fig 2.30  A floor tile demonstration*

## Demonstration

Consider the floor tiles ... one nice demonstration is that visible when viewing *nine* floor tiles where each square floor tile is decorated with *four* isosceles triangles.

# PYTHAGORAS THEOREM.

A theorem, usually attributed to Pythagoras but known to much of the Ancients worlds — was also called — the Forty Seventh Proposition (of Euclid) — the theorem of the Bride — Dulcarnon (two horned) — Carpenters Theorem — Windmill Theorem — the Franciscan Cowl. Many postage stamps honor it!

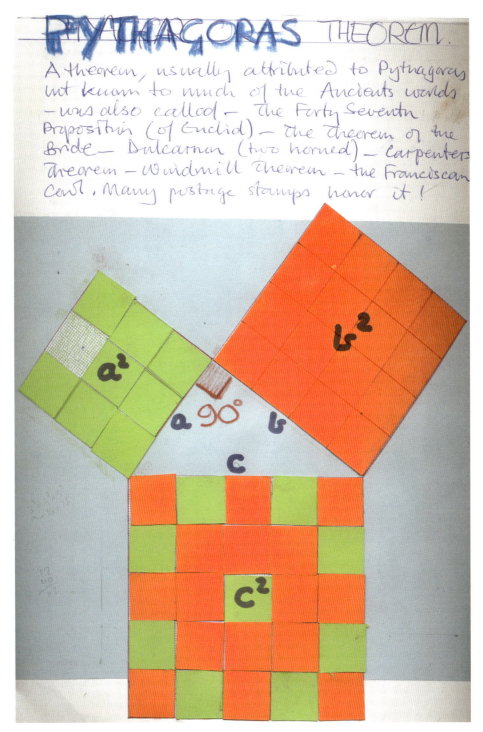

*Fig 2.31  345 Right-angle triangle*

*Exercise 34   Pythagoras 3 – 4 – 5 triangle demonstrated*

1. Draw a 3 cm × 3 cm square on yellow card.

   That is: $3^2 = 3 \times 3 = 9$

   This can be represented by a square 3 units by 3 units.

*Fig 2.32*

2. Draw a 4 cm × 4 cm square on blue card

   That is: $4^2 = 4 \times 4 = 16$

   This can be represented by a square 4 units by 4 units.

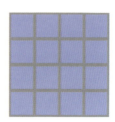

*Fig 2.33*

3. Cut the squares into nine and sixteen unit squares respectively.

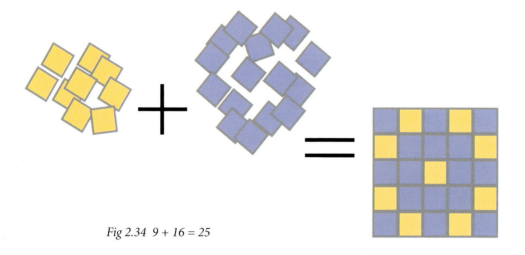

*Fig 2.34  9 + 16 = 25*

4. Let these two squares be disassembled and then the 9 plus 16 unit squares be reassembled into a single rectangle. It is found that one of these rectangles is a *square* with each side five units as in Fig 2.34.

Put these three squares together as in Fig 2.31 and it transpires that the angle opposite the *longest* side is a right-angle. We literally see that *for a right-angle triangle the sum of the squares is equal to the square on the hypotenuse.*

Hypotenuse functionally means the longest side and literally 'stretching under' from the Greek. The other two sides are called the 'legs,' or simply 'sides.'

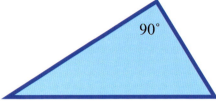

90°

*Fig 2.35 'stretching under,' hypotenuse*

There is a nice website out there there (*www.cut-the-knot.com/ pythagoras/*) by Alexander Bogomolny where fifty-four proofs of this theorem are described. The writer also mentions a book by Elisha Scott Loomis, an early twentieth-century professor, with 367 proofs of Pythagoras theorem!

## Bhaskara's proof

Most theorems have an algebraic component, so may be difficult for Class 7. One that is neat is that attributed to Bhaskara in about the year 1150. See Fig 2.37.

*Exercise 35   Bhaskara's proof of Pythagoras Theorem*

1. Take four right-angle triangles triangles all exactly the same size.

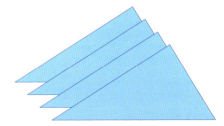

*Fig 2.36*

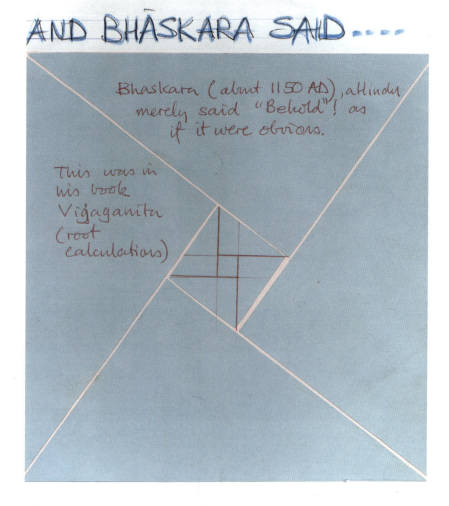

Bhaskara (about 1150 AD), a Hindu merely said "Behold"! as if it were obvious.

This was in his book Vijaganita (root calculations)

*Fig 2.37  ... and Bhaskara said 'Behold'!*

2. Now rearrange these to form a *square* where the side of the square is composed of the two different shorter legs of the initial triangles. This leaves a hole in the middle.

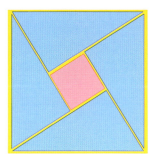

Fig 2.38

3. Label the sides of a triangle *a, b* and *c*.

4. Give the small square length *d*.

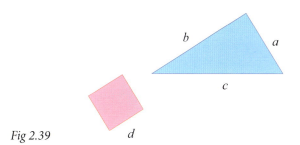

Fig 2.39

5. We note that by summing the triangles and the small square:

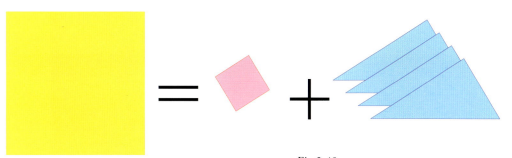

Fig 2.40

6. And that $d = b - a$ (look closely at 2 above).
   So that $d^2 = (b - a)^2$

   Also we note that the area of *one* blue triangle is $\dfrac{a \times b}{2}$

Putting the above in symbolic form we can say that:

$$c \times c = d \times d + 4\frac{(a \times b)}{2}$$

or   $c^2 = d^2 \ + \ 2ab$

thus  $c^2 = (b - a)^2 \ + 2ab$

and multiplying out we get:

$c^2 = b(b - a) \ - a(b - a) \ + 2ab$

$c^2 = b^2 - ab \ - ab + a^2 + 2ab$

$c^2 = b^2 - 2ab + a^2 + 2ab$

$c^2 = b^2 + a^2$

QED — That is: *quod erat demonstrandum* (which was to be demonstrated) or quite enough done!

Hence:    $$a^2 + b^2 = c^2$$

as the formula is usually written.

Finally some students work over the years

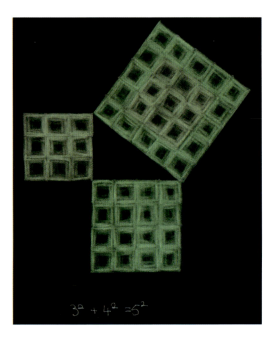

$$3^2 + 4^2 = 5^2$$

*Fig 2.41*

# PYTHAGORUS THEOREM.

A Right Angle Scalene Triangle

*Fig 2.42*

Fig 2.43

One theory is that Pythagoras discovered his famous theorem on his way to the bath...

...He saw the solution in the floor tiles of the bath house.

*Fig 2.44*

# Acknowledgments

I wish to acknowledge the many colleagues at Glenaeon Rudolf Steiner School who have conversed with me, also helped and challenged me with their expertise and interest. In our Mathematics faculty area this includes Chris Collins, Lynn Cooper and Matthew Wright, as well as an early guide — Cedric Leathbridge. This acknowledgment also includes students, some named but some not known for sure. Also I want to include a number of folk whose conversation in these areas I always enjoy in particular our old 'Morphology' group with Christel Post, David Bowden and Roger McHugh (who has now left us). They have always supported these studies. I am hugely in debt and owe the most to the individual I always regard as my teacher, Lawrence Edwards (who died in 2003), as well as to Nick Thomas and Graham Calderwood, and Andrew Hill who encouraged. Anne Jacobsen has let me use a number of her sketches and I am grateful for this.

Past students Luke Fischer and Rosie Winifred, Paul Beasly and Daniel Beasly, Yasmin Funk, Madelaine Dickie, Georgia van Toorn and Jenny Ellis have challenged and inspired. And Terry who got me some snails. And Ashley Miskelly whose sea urchin expertise astounds. And Elaine for her tree photos and introducing me to the Queen of the Night. And Ian Williams for weird meteorites. And ....

All these people have helped my research into these topics, into the patterning of things which — I believe — maths sort of is. Finally all the little things of nature which my wife Norma has noticed, brought to my attention, and added over many years, to my store of perceptions and thoughts to work with. This is apart from her patience. May this long continue!

John A Blackwood
November 2005

# Bibliography

Abbott, Edwin A. (1999, originally published 1884) *Flatland — A Romance in Many Dimensions,* Shambala, Boston and London

Alder, Ken (2002) *The Measure of all Things,* Little, Brown, London

Ball, Philip (1999) *The Self-Made Tapestry,* Oxford University Press

Bentley W A and Humfreys W J (1962 first published 1931) *Snow Crystals,* Dover Books

Blatner, David (1997) *The Joy of π,* Penguin, London

Bockemühl, Jochen (1992) *Awakening to Landscape,* Natural Science Section, The Goetheanum, Dornach, Switzerland

Bortoft, Henri (1986) *Goethe's Scientific Consciousness,* Institute for Cultural Research

— (1996) *The Wholeness of Nature,* Lindisfarne, New York, and Floris Books, Edinburgh

Casti, John L (2000) *Five More Golden Rules,* John Wiley, New York

Clegg, Brian (2003) *The First Scientist,* Constable, London

Colman, Samuel (1971, first published 1912) *Nature's Harmonic Unity,* Benjamin Blom, New York

Cook, Theodore Andreas (1979, first published 1914) *The Curves of Life,* Dover Books

Critchlow, Keith (1976) *Islamic Patterns,* Thames and Hudson, London

— (1979) *Order in Space,* Thames and Hudson, London

— (1979) *Time Stands Still,* Gordon Fraser, London, and St Martin, New York

Daintith, John and Nelson R. D., (1989) *Dictionary of Mathematics,* Penguin, London

Davidson, Norman (1985) *Astronomy and the Imagination,* Routledge, London

— (1993) *Sky Phenomena,* Lindisfarne, New York, and Floris Books, Edinburgh

Doczi, Gyorgy (1981) *The Power of Limits,* Shambala, Colorado

Eisenberg, Jerome M (1981) *Seashells of the World,* McGraw-Hill, New York

Edwards, Lawrence (1982) *The Field of Form,* Floris Books, Edinburgh

— (2002) *Projective Geometry,* Floris Books, Edinburgh

— (1993) *The Vortex of Life,* Floris Books, Edinburgh

Endres, Klaus-Peter and Schad, Wolfgang (1997) *Moon Rhythms in Nature,* Floris Books, Edinburgh


Folley, Tom and Zaczek, Iain (1998) *The Book of the Sun,* New Burlington, London


Gaarder, Jostein (1995) *Sophie's World,* Phoenix House, London

Garland, Trudi Hammel, *Fascinating Fibonaccis,* Dale Seymour, New York

Ghyka, Matila (1977) *The Geometry of Art and Life,* Dover Books, New York

Gleick, James (1987) *Chaos,* Penguin Books, New York

Golubitsky, Martin and Stewart, Ian (1992) *Fearful Symmetry,* Blackwell, Oxford

Goodwin, Brian (1994) *How the Leopard Changed Its Spots,* Weidenfeld and Nicholson, London

Guedj, Denis (1996) *Numbers: The Universal Language,* Thames and Hudson, London

Gullberg, Jan (1997) *Mathematics, From The Birth Of Numbers,* Norton, New York


Hawking, Stephen (2001) *The Universe in a Nutshell,* Bantam, London

Heath, Thomas L. (1926) *The Thirteen Books of Euclid,* Cambridge University Press

Hoffman, Paul (1998) *The Man Who Loved Only Numbers,* Fourth Estate, London

Holdrege, Craig (2002) *The Dynamic Heart and Circulation,* AWSNA, Fair Oaks

Hoyle, Fred (1962) *Astronomy,* Macdonald, London

Huntley, H. E. (1970) *The Divine Proportion,* Dover Books


Kollar, L. Peter (1983) *Form,* privately published, Sydney

Kuiter, Rudie H (1996) *Guide to Sea Fishes of Australia,* New Holland, Sydney

Livio, Mario (2002) *The Golden Ratio,* Review, London

Lovelock, James (1988) *The Ages of Gaia,* Oxford University Press

Maor, Eli (1994) *The Story of a Number,* Princeton University Press

Mandelbrot, Benoit B (1977) *The Fractal Geometry of Nature,* W. H. Freeman, New York

Mankiewicz, Richard (2000) *The Story of Mathematics,* Cassell, London

Marti, Ernst (1984) *The Four Ethers,* Schaumberg Publications, Roselle, Illinois

Miskelly. Ashley (2002) *Sea Urchins of Australia and the Indo-Pacific,* Capricornia Publications, Sydney

Moore, Patrick and Nicholson Iain (1985) *The Universe,* Collins, London

Nahin, Paul J (1998) *The Story of $\sqrt{-1}$,* Princetown University Press

Pakenham, Thomas (1996) *Remarkable Trees of the World,* Weidenfeld & Nicolson, London

Peterson, Ivars (1990) *Islands of Truth,* W. H. Freeman, New York

Peterson, Ivars (1988) *The Mathematical Tourist,* W. H. Freeman, New York

Plato, *Timaeus*

Posamentier, Alfred S, and Lehmann, Ingmar (2004) *A Biography of the World's Most Mysterious Number,* Prometheus Books, New York

Richter, Gottfried (1982) *Art and Human Consciousness,* Anthroposophic Press, New York, and Floris Books, Edinburgh

Ruskin, John (1971, originally 1857) *The Elements of Drawing,* Dover Books

Saward, Jeff (2003) *Labyrinths & Mazes,* Gaia Books, Stroud

Schwenk, Theodor (1965) *Sensitive Chaos,* Rudolf Steiner Press, London

Sheldrake, Rupert (1985) *A New Science of Life,* Anthony Blond, London

Sobel, Dava (2005) *The Planets,* Fourth Estate, London

Steiner, Rudolf (1984, originally 1923) *The Cycle of the Year,* Anthroposophical Press, New York

— (1972, originally 1920) *Man: Hieroglyph of the Universe,* Rudolf Steiner Press, London

— (1960, originally 1922) *Human Questions and Cosmic Answers,* Anthroposophical Publishing Company, London

— (1991, originally 1914) *Human and Cosmic Thought,* Rudolf Steiner Press, London

— (1947, lectures given in December 1918) *How can Mankind find the Christ again,* Anthroposophic Press, New York

— (1961) *Mission of the Archangel Michael,* 6 lectures given in Dornach, Switzerland, in 1919, Anthroposophic Press, New York, USA

— (1997, originally 1910) *An Outline of Esoteric Science,* Anthroposophic Press, New York

— *The Relation of the Diverse branches of Natural Science to Astronomy,* 18 lectures given in Stuttgart, Germany, in 1921

— (1983) *The Search for the New Isis, Divine Sophia,* Mercury Press, New York

Stevens, Peter S. (1974) *Patterns in Nature,* Penguin, New York

Stewart, Ian (1989) *Does God Play Dice,* Penguin

— (1998) *Life's Other Secret,* Penguin

Stewart, Ian (2001) *What Shape is a Snowflake?* Weidenfeld and Nicolson, London

Stockmeyer, E.A.K (1969) *Rudolf Steiner's Curriculum for Waldorf Schools,* Steiner Schools Fellowship

Strauss, Michaela (1978) *Understanding Children's Drawings,* Rudolf Steiner Press, London


Tacey, David (2003) *The Spirituality Revolution,* Harper Collins, Sydney

Thomas, Nick (1999) *Science between Space and Counterspace,* Temple Lodge Books, London

Thompson, D'Arcy Wentworth (1992, originally 1916) *On Growth and Form,* Dover Books


Van Romunde, Dick (2001) *About Formative Forces in the Plant World,* Jannebeth Roell, New York

Wachsmuth, Guenther (1927) *The Etheric Formative Forces in Cosmos, Earth and Man*, New York

Wells, David (1986) *The Penguin Book of Curious and Interesting Numbers,* London

Wolfram, Stephen (2002) *A New Kind of Science,* Wolfram Media

Whicher, Olive (1952) *The Plant Between Sun and Earth,* Rudolf Steiner Press, London

— (1971) *Projective Geometry,* Rudolf Steiner Press, London

— (1989) *Sunspace,* Rudolf Steiner Press, London

Zajonc, Arthur, (1993) *Catching the Light,* Bantam, New York

# Index

# Mathematics in Space and Time

The sequel to *Mathematics Around Us,* suitable for Year 8 in the Steiner-Waldorf Education curriculum, investigates Platonic Solids, and rhythms and cycles in nature.

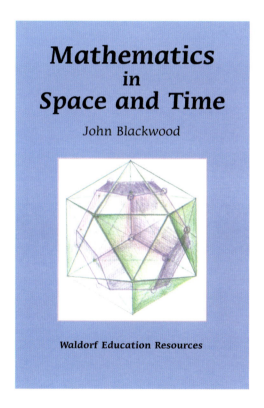

www.florisbooks.co.uk

Jack Petrash

# Understanding Waldorf Education

A jargon-free view of Waldorf education and its philosophy of a three-dimensional education.

Since their inception over 80 years ago, Steiner-Waldorf Schools have offered a much-needed model for educational reform. The author provides a compelling, clearly written picture of the key components of a Waldorf education, focusing especially on child learning experiences that develop thought, feeling, and intentional, purposeful activity.

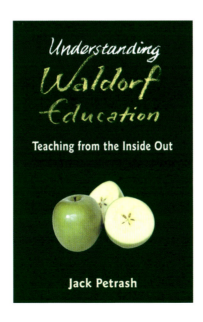

www.florisbooks.co.uk

Also in the Waldorf Education Resources series:

Charles Kovacs

# Ancient Rome

This book, for use by Steiner-Waldorf teachers, includes stories of the founding of Rome, the early battles with Carthage and Hannibal, Julius Caesar and the conquests of Gaul and Britain, Antony and Cleopatra, and the decline and fall under the Huns and the beginning of the Dark Ages.

It is recommended for Steiner-Waldorf curriculum Class 6 (age 11–12).

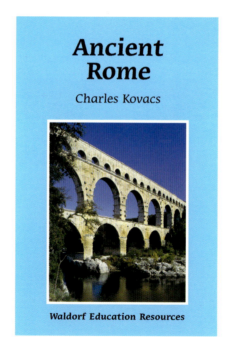

www.florisbooks.co.uk

Also in the Waldorf Education Resources series:

Charles Kovacs

# Botany

Charles Kovacs characterizes different plants, from fungi, algae
and lichens, to the lily and rose families. He describes the parts
of each plant and their growth cycle.

It is recommended for Steiner-Waldorf curriculum Class 5-6
(age 10–12).

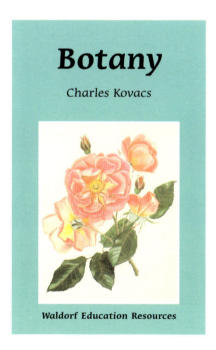

www.florisbooks.co.uk

Lawrence Edwards

# Projective Geometry

Lawrence Edwards researched and taught projective geometry for more than forty years. Here, he presents a clear and artistic understanding of the intriguing qualities of non-Euclidian geometry. Illustrated with over 200 instructive diagrams and exercises, this book will reveal the secrets of space to those who work through them. A valuable resource for Steiner-Waldorf teachers.

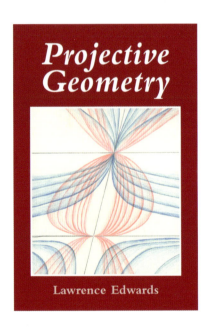

www.florisbooks.co.uk

Lawrence Edwards

# The Vortex of Life

When *The Vortex of Life* was first published in 1993, Lawrence Edwards's pioneering work on bud shapes had already attracted the attention of many scientists around the world. In the book, Edwards gave a fuller account of his research, widening it to include the forms of plants, embryos and organs such as the heart.

His work suggests that there are universal laws, not yet fully understood, which guide an organism's growth into predetermined patterns. His work has profound implications for those working in genetics and stem-cell research.

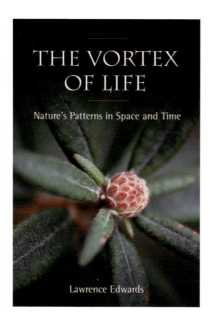

THE VORTEX OF LIFE

Nature's Patterns in Space and Time

Lawrence Edwards

www.florisbooks.co.uk